Baroque sites
in Italy

D1630185

YUGOSLAVIA

● TRIESTE

● SPLIT

ADRIATIC SEA

ITALY

ME
astelgandolfo
Ariccia

Bari ●

● NAPLES

● Salerno

● Taranto   Lecce ●

YRRHENIAN SEA

Great Buildings of the World

Baroque Churches

by P. and C. Cannon-Brookes

Paul Hamlyn
London. New York. Sydney. Toronto

Endpapers: Maps showing the sites of Baroque churches mentioned in the text.

Frontispiece: Stucco figures of fishermen and putti by Antonio Raggi from the church of S. Andrea al Quirinale.

Published by
The Hamlyn Publishing Group Limited
London · New York · Sydney · Toronto
Hamlyn House, The Centre, Feltham, Middlesex

© The Hamlyn Publishing Group Limited 1969

Printed and bound in Great Britain by
Morrison and Gibb Limited, London and Edinburgh

Contents

Introduction

Today, by common consent, the term Baroque is applied loosely to the art of the 17th and 18th centuries; it therefore tends to have as much a chronological significance as a stylistic one. At first Baroque was a term of abuse, probably deriving in Italy from the word *baroco*, which was used by medieval philosophers to describe an obstacle in schematic logic and consequently came to describe any contorted idea or involuted process of thought. It seems also to be partly derived from the Portuguese *barroco*, or the Spanish *barrueco*, meaning an irregular or imperfectly shaped pearl. However, by the middle of the 18th century, the term began to be applied to art in a less derogatory fashion.

It is given three meanings in the French *Dictionnaire des Travaux* of 1771, first as a technical term used by jewellers and secondly as irregular, bizarre or unequal. (To this day, jewellers still refer to large irregular pearls as 'baroque' pearls.) The third meaning is closely related to the previous two since a picture or a figure is said to be painted in the 'baroque' style if rules and proportions are not observed and everything is depicted according to the artist's whim. This is of course a Neo-Classical view of the preceding style, and with the rise of the Neo-Classical movement the term came to be used to describe a specific type of 'degeneration' in the arts characterised by an opposition to or disregard of the particular values cherished by the antiquarian Winckelmann and his followers.

The application of the word in this sense continued into the 19th century until Heinrich Wölfflin in his pioneer study *Renaissance und Barock* of 1888 used it for stylistic analysis rather than as a thinly veiled term of abuse. Nevertheless, apart from a minority of German scholars and the occasional enthusiast, prejudice against Baroque art remained strong in Britain and the United States until

The façade of the Gesù, Rome, by Giacomo della Porta, 1575. The austerity and flatness of the façade, with very little variation in depth over its width and an almost timid articulation with plain pilasters, are characteristic of the generation of architects before Carlo Maderno. 9

well after the Second World War. Baroque art probably reached its nadir during the war years when the wholesale destruction of Baroque churches in Italy by allied bombing caused hardly a raised eyebrow. During the 1950s a remarkable resurgence of interest in Baroque art took place, to which Rudolf Wittkower's book *Art and Architecture in Italy: 1600–1750* was probably the most important single contribution.

Because of the complexity of the period to which such a loosely defined term is applied, it is necessary to make the meaning more precise by the addition of prefixes, or else the range of production covered by the simple term will render it almost meaningless. These subdivisions, such as Early Baroque, High Baroque, Late Baroque, Classical Baroque and so on, are much more closely defined both stylistically and chronologically, and they will, where

Opposite, the interior of the Gesù. To accommodate the vast congregations attracted by the Jesuits, Vignola employed a Latin cross design with a short wide nave, shallow transepts and choir, and a dome over the central area to provide plenty of light, so that every member of the congregation could hear the preacher clearly. The rich frescoes and gilding belong to a later phase of the Counter Reformation, and were executed by G. B. Gaulli in the late 17th century.

Left, the façade of S. Susanna, Rome, built by Carlo Maderno, 1597–1603. In his design there is a progressive movement and concentration of decoration towards the centre of the façade. The bays become increasingly wider and are placed one in front of the other leading to the climax of the entrance, while the scrolls are tighter and more dynamic than those on the Gesù, and the overall effect is strongly sculptural.

Above, St Peter's, Rome. The dome designed by Michelangelo was heavily modified by Giacomo della Porta after 1564; Carlo Maderno began the nave and façade in 1607 and Bernini's splendid colonnades were added later from 1656.

Below, the tiny façade of S. Bibiana, Rome, begun by Bernini in 1624. The forceful handling of the elements and their intricate dynamic balance are much more highly developed than in the Early Baroque façade of S. Susanna and it is this dynamic quality which characterises High Baroque architecture.

possible, be used in preference to the simple term in this book. However, it must be emphasised immediately that any such divisions are purely devices of the critic, erected for convenience on stylistic grounds, and they have no greater significance than to help clarify the great number of stylistic variations of the period.

Linked with Baroque is Rococo, and this style appears considerably later in time. The word is probably derived from the French *rocaille*, used to describe shell and pebble work in 16th-century decoration. This term came into more general use in the late 18th century in Paris as a nickname for the style against which the Neo-Classical artists were revolting. The Rococo is not so much an autonomous style as a facet of the Late Baroque, standing in very much the same relationship to it as Mannerism does to High Renaissance. Rococo decoration reached its peak in France in the period around 1730, but the French predilection towards classicism meant that although the Rococo style remained dominant in the fields of the applied arts throughout most of the 18th century, classicism rapidly reasserted itself in the fields of architecture and formal sculpture. Undoubtedly the most brilliant developments in Rococo decoration took place not in France but in Central and Eastern Europe, where it remained the dominant style for most of the century. Increasing restraint is felt after about 1760 under the influence of the growing Neo-Classical movement, though the two styles co-existed for several decades until the Rococo became a purely popular art form in Germany and Eastern Europe at the end of the 18th century.

The transformation of Rome into the Baroque city we now know was begun under Pope Sixtus V (1485–89) when he employed Domenico Fontana to replan much of the city. He was responsible for building many new streets linking churches and piazzas, and to give a focal point to several of his designs he moved ancient obelisks to important positions, such as the Piazza di San Pietro and the Piazza del Popolo. However, his nephew and pupil Carlo Maderno (1556–1629) was a much more resourceful architect and his work characterises the Early Baroque in Rome. Maderno's earliest building there marks the transition from the severity and dry classicism of the previous generation of architects including Giacomo della Porta, Ponzio and Fontana himself, towards the richness and ebullience of the High Baroque. The key work is the façade of the small church of S. Susanna (built in 1597–1603),

Bernini's S. Maria dell'Assunzione at Ariccia, begun in 1662. The simple cylindrical body of the church, crowned by a hemispherical dome, is in dramatic contrast to the long low wings almost enclosing it.

which is a direct parallel in architecture to the frescoes by Annibale Carracci in the Palazzo Farnese.

In 1603 Maderno was appointed 'Architect to St Peter's' and to him fell the task of completing the main structural work. At the death of Michelangelo in 1564 the drum of the dome was almost complete, but in the following years Giacomo della Porta drastically altered its design. Instead of the strictly classical hemispherical dome intended by Michelangelo he designed a pointed dome, which considerably reduced the engineering problems inherent in the structure. Paul V decided to abandon Michelangelo's centrally planned design and in 1607 Maderno began work on both the nave and the façade. For the design of the nave interior he was to a great extent tied to Michelangelo's choir and transepts and as a result the nave is something of a compromise solution. The design of the façade also presented problems since it had to be kept low so that Michelangelo's dome should not be obscured, and the famous Benediction Loggia had to be included on a scale small enough not to dwarf the pope. With these problems in mind Maderno abandoned the two-storey type of façade and instead turned for inspiration to the palace type of façade, in particular to Michelangelo's palaces on the Capitol.

Remarkably, with the sole exception of S. Maria in Campitelli, all the most important and influential High Baroque churches in Rome are relatively small. This is perhaps less surprising when it is remembered that by the late 1620s the new orders were all well supplied with enormous churches, and that St Peter's for over half the century dominated papal expenditure on religious buildings. The four leading architects of the High Baroque in Rome were Gianlorenzo Bernini (1598–1680), Pietro da Cortona (1596–1669), Francesco Borromini (1599–1667) and Carlo Rainaldi (1611–1691), of which Bernini is undoubtedly the best known.

Bernini, like Michangelo, was an extremely versatile genius, and although originally trained as a sculptor, he was a highly successful architect and a painter of no mean standing. To this may be added his great qualities as a courtier and administrator, so it is understandable why he has left a greater mark on Rome than any other single artist. His architectural activity began in the early 1620s, when he worked on the Palazzo Barberini under Maderno and in 1629, on Maderno's death, he succeeded him to the post of 'Architect to St Peter's'; it is Bernini's embellishments to both the interior 14 and exterior of the basilica that make it one of the greatest High

The Cornaro Chapel in S. Maria della Vittoria, Rome, was decorated by Bernini in 1645–52 when he was temporarily out of papal favour. The rich white marble group of St Teresa in ecstasy floats in front of a richly coloured marble background, while light floods down the gilt bronze rays from a concealed source above. In 'opera' boxes on each side of the chapel members of the Cornaro family, carved from white marble, witness the ecstasy of the saint, and the worshipper joins them. This dramatic breakdown of the traditional boundaries between painting, sculpture and architecture to produce an overwhelming theatrical illusion found few followers in Italy. Bernini's natural successors were the Asam brothers in southern Germany.

Above, the interior of the dome of Pietro da Cortona's SS. Martina e Luca, Rome, completed in 1650.

Left, the façade of SS. Martina e Luca showing the intricate overlapping and interpenetration of elements which gives it a strongly organic quality, while the dynamic balance between the gently bowed central section and the sharply delineated side pieces is typically High Baroque.

Above right, the façade of S. Maria della Pace by Pietro da Cortona.

Below right, the façade of S. Carlo alle Quattro Fontane, Rome, by Francesco Borromini, almost completed by 1667. The convex form of the central bay of the lower storey is carried up into the second storey in the form of an oval 'sentry box' topped by a squat onion dome, which acts as a subtle transition between the two storeys.

Baroque monuments in Rome. In 1624 Bernini also began working on the tiny façade of S. Bibiana, which is a landmark in the evolution of High Baroque architecture.

The three other churches by Bernini, S. Tomaso di Villanova at Castelgandolfo, S. Maria della Assunzione at Ariccia and S. Andrea al Quirinale, all date from the latter part of his career and all employ centralised plans. S. Tomaso (1658–61) is based on a simple Greek cross plan, almost reminiscent of Guiliano da Sangallo's S. Maria delle Carceri, but in comparison to such Renaissance churches the increased height and the dominance of the dome are Baroque characteristics. The richness of the decoration of the dome is in complete contrast to the austerity of the remainder of the church, and unlike the similar domes in Bernini's other two late churches the stucco figures support oval bas-reliefs depicting incidents in the life of the saint. S. Andrea al Quirinale is perhaps the most highly developed of the three and is discussed in greater detail later. S. Maria dell' Assunzione at Ariccia, built for the Chigis in 1662–64, is also an extremely subtle and influential church, but Bernini's interest in illusionism is most clearly seen in two much smaller works, the decoration of the Cornaro Chapel in S. Maria della Vittoria and the Altieri Chapel in S. Francesco a Ripa.

Curiously none of the major architects active in Rome during the 17th century was a native of the city. Bernini's father was Florentine while his mother was Neapolitan, and Pietro da Cortona was, as his name suggests, a Tuscan by birth. Like Bernini he was not only an architect but also an important painter, and his gigantic frescoes in the Palazzo Barberini and in S. Maria in Vallicella identify him as the most important monumental painter of the High Baroque. His church architecture represents a completely different stream to that of Bernini since his work was deeply rooted in the Tuscan tradition, and his most important church, Ss. Martina e Luca, was completed in 1650. In 1634 he had been given permission to rebuild the crypt of the church of the Academy of St Luke in order to provide a tomb for himself, but during the excavations they discovered the remains of S. Martina, which led Cardinal Francesco Barberini to commission the rebuilding of the entire church.

The façade is a complete break with the Roman tradition in that it consists of two equal storeys and the central section is gently curved. Inside the church the structure of the lower storey of the façade is repeated in a slightly different key with orders of the same

Groundplan of S. Carlo alle Quattro Fontane with its surrounding monastic buildings, showing the extremely small site available to Borromini.

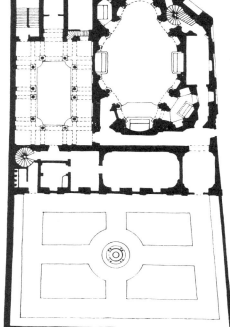

size so that a complete homogeneity is created between the interior and the exterior. The plan is based on a Greek cross with apsidal endings to the arms, and the wall surfaces are completely broken up into three different planes, partly by the use of screening columns and pilasters. This gives the walls an undulating rhythm, which is enhanced by the lack of colour in the interior, all of which is a crisp white. In contrast to the severity of the lower part of the interior, the vaults are richly decorated with elaborately patterned coffering, and the design of the dome and semi-domes is particularly interesting. The strange rippling curvilinear design of the coffering is without parallel; Pietro da Cortona has also superimposed a system of ribs

18

in order to control the upward movement and so produced a synthesis of the Roman tradition of coffering with the Northern tradition of ribs, which was rapidly taken up by other architects including Bernini.

Pietro da Cortona's later works have an increasing massiveness and grandeur, which is clearly seen in his modernisation of the façade of S. Maria della Pace (1656–57). The convex upper storey repeats in a slightly simplified form the upper storey of the facade of Ss. Martina e Luca, though the system of interpenetrating elements is even more complicated and the Michelangelesque quality of the pediment is strongly pronounced. However below there is a boldly projecting semicircular portico, which reveals him experimenting with the theme that so interested Bernini and Borromini. A reflection of this portico is found in England in the porticos of the transepts of St Paul's Cathedral.

One of the greatest Roman High Baroque architects was Francesco Borromini and he could not have been more different from Bernini. For while Bernini was the brilliant extrovert and immensely successful, Borromini was neurotic and a recluse. Bernini regarded painting and sculpture as an adequate preparation for his architecture, but Borromini had been trained as a builder and architectural draughtsman and was a superb technician. It is

The interior of S. Carlo alle Quattro Fontane. The massive columns are arranged in groups of four with larger intervals on the longitudinal and transverse axes. This arrangement gives two possible rhythms, depending on whether the longitudinal and transverse axes are felt to predominate. In fact neither predominates, and the complexities in the planning are held under control by the heavy entablature which undulates round the perimeter of the church.

thus not altogether surprising that their approaches to architecture should have differed so drastically. Borromini was born in 1599 at Bissone on Lake Lugano and by tradition he worked briefly in Milan before settling in Rome about 1620. There, his first independent work was the construction of the church and monastery of S. Carlo alle Quattro Fontane for the Spanish Discalced Trinitarians (commissioned in 1634). The tiny church was begun in 1638 and with the exception of the façade it was completed by 1641. However, it is in the planning of this church that the full contrast between Borromini and Bernini becomes apparent. Throughout his architecture Bernini remained faithful to the classical anthropomorphic tradition of planning in terms of modules, but in S. Carlo and S. Ivo della Sapienza (begun 1642) Borromini abandoned this system and instead used a non-anthropomorphic system based on angles. In S. Carlo the geometrical basis of the final plan was a diamond formed of two equilateral triangles with a common base along the transverse axis of the building; from this axis a series of arcs were drawn to obtain the outline of the groundplan. Further, the location of the sixteen massive columns which articulate the walls was determined on a basis of angular relationships.

The façade of S. Carlo was not erected until the very end of Borromini's life and apart from sculptural decorations, it was completed in the year of his death, 1667. Here he designed a façade of two storeys of three bays, almost equal in height, but while in the lower storey a convex bay in the centre is flanked by concave bays, the upper storey consists of three concave bays. The interplay of curves and sharp angles and the unexpected juxtapositions of bizarre elements give this façade an intensely lively quality, which exploits fully the narrow street in which it is located.

Carlo Rainaldi was half a generation younger than the great trio already discussed, but after them he was undoubtedly the most outstanding architect in Rome. His importance lies in his introduction of the North Italian scenographic tradition stemming from Palladio. In so doing, he achieved a remarkable synthesis between complex Mannerist planning and the dynamism of the High Baroque. His borrowings and adaptations of ideas derived from the great trio are completely transformed into a strong personal style, and in the formation of this the influence of his father was considerable. Girolamo Rainaldi was trained under Fontana, and his rather weak, retardataire style met with limited success in Rome, but during his long career he spent extended

Above, the façade of S. Maria in Campitelli, Rome, built by Carlo Rainaldi, 1663–67. The strongly projecting sections of entablature supported by columns are reminiscent of Late Classical architecture, but with Rainaldi the forms are handled much more emphatically, the broken pediment is thrust vigorously outwards against the skyline, and the massive columns give the façade a rich solemnity.

Right, the interior of S. Maria in Campitelli. Rainaldi articulated the side chapels with gigantic Corinthian columns while the nave space proper is articulated with pilasters alone, thus creating a strong transverse axis across the body of the church. But the same massive columns are repeated framing the entrance to the choir, and again framing the sanctuary, so an equally strong link is formed along the longitudinal axis between the three almost separate spaces. The system of lighting with the dark nave, brilliantly lit choir and dark sanctuary point to the influence of Palladio.

periods in Northern Italy, in particular Bologna, Parma, Piacenza and Modena. There he came into close contact with the North Italian tradition and passed it on to his son Carlo.

The scenographic qualities of Rainaldi's S. Maria in Campitelli (1663–67) make it unique among the High Baroque churches of Rome and its system of planning is much closer to that of Longhena's Salute than the churches of Bernini or Borromini. The longitudinal nave opens at each side into large chapels flanked by a pair of smaller chapels, and leads through a gigantic archway into a domed choir and a semicircular apsidal sanctuary. Such a layout is typically North Italian and can be paralleled closely, for example, in Magenta's church of S. Salvatore in Bologna (1605–23), but compared to S. Salvatore the side chapels are much more strongly emphasised and much greater use is made of the lighting.

In the last quarter of the 17th century the architectural centre of gravity moves from Rome to Northern Italy and in particular to Piedmont, while during the middle of the century the only architect outside Rome comparable to the four already discussed is Longhena. Baldassare Longhena (1598–1682) was an almost exact contemporary of Bernini, but his masterpiece, the great church of S. Maria della Salute in Venice (which is discussed in detail later), shows him to be the heir to Palladio and the North Italian scenographic tradition. Apart from the façade of the little Chiesa dell'Ospedaletto in Venice (1650–58) and the brilliant staircase in the monastery of S. Giorgio Maggiore, he is best known as a builder of palaces, which are very subdued by Roman standards.

The arrival of Guarino Guarini in Turin in 1666 at the invitation of Charles Emmanuel II marks a new era of Baroque architecture in Piedmont, just at the moment when the overwhelming influence of Rome was beginning to decline. Over a century of enlightened patronage provided the basis for the remarkable flowering of Piedmontese architecture, and it was dominated by the three architects Guarino Guarini, Filippo Juvarra and Bernardo Vittone. Guarini himself was a native of Modena; he entered the Theatine Order at the age of 15 in 1639 and was partly trained in Rome. There he studied theology, philosophy, mathematics and architecture and was undoubtedly drawn to the latest achievements of Borromini.

Although in certain aspects Guarini proved to be the natural successor to Borromini, his mature works break away entirely from
the Roman Baroque tradition, especially in his rejection of the

Left, the interior of the Carmine, Turin, built by Filippo Juvarra, 1732–35. Instead of large clerestory windows over the side chapel entrances as in S. Maria in Campitelli, the entrance arch of each chapel extends right up into the barrel vault, and arch-shaped cresting is inserted mid-way, which defines the chapel proper and creates a deep gallery above. This means that the wall as the visual boundary of the nave has been replaced by a skeleton of high pillars, which is fundamentally a Gothic scheme and clearly derives from the north.

Juvarra's ecclesiastical masterpiece, the Superga, was built on a magnificent site overlooking Turin, 1717–31. The structure of the church is half-buried within the monastery buildings in a manner strongly reminiscent of the great northern monasteries such as Ettal and Melk.

solid classical type of dome in favour of a skeletal diaphanous structure. He planned his churches, like Borromini, on a non-anthropomorphic and geometrical basis with particular emphasis on the interpenetration of spatial units, while his wall surfaces, as such, tend to almost disappear behind a maze of structural elements. Guarini the mathematician is revealed in the intricate symbolism included in the planning of his churches, while it is, perhaps, the mathematical precision of his forms and his extraordinary grasp of engineering, pushing the materials to their extreme limits, which makes Guarini's architecture so fascinating to contemporary architects and engineers.

Filippo Juvarra did not arrive in Turin until 31 years after the death of Guarini, and his buildings show an almost complete break with Guarini's style. Juvarra had been trained in Rome under Carlo Fontana and had based his architectural style on the rather academic Late Baroque style current in Rome at the time. However, he possessed an immensely fertile imagination and these Late Baroque ideas were completely transformed in the bold stage designs he produced for Cardinal Ottoboni from 1708. His great chance came in 1714 when he was invited to enter the service of Victor Amadeo II of Savoy, first at his birthplace Messina and very shortly afterwards in Turin. Throughout the remainder of his career Juvarra continued to pour out stage and applied-art designs and these interests are reflected in his architecture. Some idea of his productivity can be gained from the list of his major works in or near Turin alone, which includes five large churches, four royal palaces, four other important palaces, and the overall design of two whole quarters of the city, all achieved in 22 years. His services were also in demand outside Piedmont, and in 1719–20 he spent a year in Portugal followed by visits to London and Paris, while in 1735 he was given leave to go to Madrid to design a new royal palace for Philip V and died there the following year.

Stylistically Juvarra was eclectic for he tended to choose his style to suit the commission, and the contrast between the theatrical effect of Stupinigi and the echoes of Versailles in the façade of Palazzo Madama in Turin could not be greater. The entire previous evolution of Italian architecture provided sources of inspiration for Juvarra, but more important still, he was the first major Italian architect to turn also to Northern and even Gothic architecture. Thus in his work is to be seen not only the final culmination of the Italian classical tradition stemming from the Renaissance, but also

The south transept of St Paul's Cathedral, London, showing the porch probably derived from Pietro da Cortona's S. Maria della Pace in Rome. The cool classicism displayed by Sir Christopher Wren is closer in spirit to Inigo Jones and to contemporary French architecture than to the dramatic dynamism of the Roman High Baroque.

the seeds of its dissolution. These exotic influences become stronger at the end of his career, as is obvious when his church of S. Filippo Neri in Turin of 1715 is compared to the Carmine of 1732–35.

Juvarra's ecclesiastical masterpiece is undoubtedly the Superga, which was built on the top of a high hill overlooking Turin in 1717–31. This complex comprises a large centrally planned church attached to a long, low rectangular monastery. The high cylindrical body of the church is half-buried in the monastery but the remainder protrudes out in front of the pair of towers and the whole is crowned by a tall and elegant dome. The grand pantheon-type portico is absolutely simple and emphasises the height and elegance of the dome behind, while the church is set on a podium approached by flights of stairs on three sides. Juvarra handled the interior with the same emphasis on elegance and sophistication, and the octagonal design of the lowermost storey is transformed into the circular design of the drum by the brilliantly simple expedient of carrying the drum on a heavy ring entablature, which is in turn carried by the eight columns at the corners of the octagon. The ring also just touches the tops of the four arches leading into the altar sanctuary, the entrance space and the two principal side altars, thus com-

B.C.—2

bining the two storeys into a single structure of extraordinary purity and simplicity. The altar sanctuary, following the North Italian tradition, is relatively small and has its own small dome, which is not reflected in the exterior of the building, while the simple sophistication of the church with its dominant colours of white and pale yellow is maintained in the enormous white marble reliefs over the altars. The effect of the interior of the church is thoroughly Italian, but the relationship between the church and the monastery is wholly non-Italian and immediately brings to mind Northern examples, particularly Melk (begun 1702).

The third important Piedmontese architect was Bernardo Vittone (1704/5–1770) and unlike Guarini and Juvarra he was born in Piedmont. Although Vittone is perhaps not as well known, his buildings are highly imaginative and it is only their relative inaccessibility that has prevented their recognition. Vittone studied in Rome, winning first prize at the Accademia di San Luca in 1732, and on his return to Turin he was asked by the Theatines, who had inherited Guarini's papers, to edit Guarini's *Architettura Civile*. (A shortened version had been published under the title *Dissegni d'architettura civile et ecclesiastica* in Turin in 1686 but the full text including extensive sections on a new type of spherical geometry was not published until this edition of 1737.) This literary work clearly had great influence on Vittone's approach to architecture and probably explains why Vittone's earliest known building, the little sanctuary at Vallinotto, is such an accomplished essay in the Guarinesque idiom. The exterior of the sanctuary has the pagoda-like tiers characteristic of the Guarinesque tradition, but in contrast to Guarini's own churches the handling of the exterior is extreme in its simplicity, and all Guarini's profusion of decorative elements is rejected (probably under the influence of Juvarra) in favour of an absolutely plain clear-cut structure. Inside further differences are to be seen: the diaphanous Guarinesque dome leads on to a double cut-off dome topped by a cupola and, in contrast to Guarini, who always clearly separated the zones, the structure of the body of the church is carried on upwards, without any break, into the diaphanous dome zone. This gives, in effect, a total of four different vaults seen one through the other, and Guarini's solemn Baroque qualities have given way to the much lighter and vivacious Rococo qualities of Vittone.

Vittone's later churches such as S. Chiara at Brà of 1742 carry on these ideas, and at Brà Vittone developed the scheme of a central

Lemercier's Church of the Sorbonne, Paris, begun in 1635. Compared with St Paul's, the forms have a clarity and intellectual precision which gives French 17th-century classicism its unique character.

Left, the Michaelskirche, Munich, begun by Friedrich Sustris in 1583. The basic design of this church follows traditional Gothic types, but the Italianate decoration is fully coherent and organised with considerable sophistication for its date.

Below, the façade of Salzburg Cathedral, designed by Santino Solari and built 1614–28. The first purely Italian church to be built north of the Alps, its façade echoes Maderno's plans for the façade of St Peter's.

circular space with four segmental chapels forming a quatrefoil. As at Valinotto, the device of Juvarra's galleries in the Carmine in Turin is applied to the centrally planned structure, but now the vaults above all four galleries are pierced with oculi through which are seen further painted vaults. Vittone's other important contribution was his invention of the inverted squinch in the church of the Ospizio di Carità at Carignano (before 1749). Here the piers of the crossing carry a pendentive zone, which in turn carries the ribbed dome divided into eight compartments, but Vittone placed deep arches and windows on the diagonal axes of the dome and then scalloped out the majority of the pendentive below to form an inverted squinch. This results in the curious situation whereby the square plan of the lowermost zone passes into a broken circle at the top of the pendentive zone and then back into a distorted octagonal dome. Vittone's pupils and followers carried on this tradition until the close of the 18th century and the triumph of Neo-Classicism.

From the frame of reference provided by the preceding account it is possible to analyse Northern churches of the 17th century, and to make a distinction between the *Baroque* churches built in

Northern Europe during the 17th century and 17th-century Northern churches in general. This distinction may seem pedantic but it is essential in order to preserve a consistent meaning for the word Baroque throughout this book, and to differentiate between the Baroque and the merely Italianate. There is a very great deal of 17th-century Italianate architecture in Northern Europe, as well as in Spain and Portugal, but compared to Italy there are almost no surviving High Baroque churches north of the Alps. Those 17th-century churches in Northern Europe that do show characteristics of the Baroque style as previously defined all tend to belong to the classicising streams, and it is not until the 18th century that the *mouvementé* qualities of Italian High Baroque architecture began to be exploited in the North. Spain and Portugal remained throughout the 17th century a law unto themselves and in most instances vast quantities of Italian Baroque motifs were applied on to structures that were at the best Italianate, and often more Gothic, in spirit.

England was very well provided with Gothic churches and with few exceptions there was little demand for new churches in any numbers until the Industrial Revolution and the enormous rise in population of the 18th century. The most important exception was the massive rebuilding programme of City churches resulting from the Great Fire of London in 1666, and outside the cities 17th-century churches are relative rarities. In the period before the Civil War Inigo Jones imported into England a relatively pure Italianate style, but this was derived almost entirely from Palladio and his followers and was thus fundamentally a Late Renaissance rather than Baroque style. The strong classicism of Inigo Jones's architecture made its impression on Sir Christopher Wren, the dominant British architect after the Restoration of 1660, and continues through the work of Nicholas Hawksmoor and James Gibbs, though often with more exotic additions.

French churches of the 17th century are again surprisingly few in number and extremely restrained in their handling. The façade of St Gervais in Paris, by Salomon de Brosse of 1616, with its three-storey design, looks back to Lescot's frontispieces in the Cour Carrée of the Louvre (begun 1546), but just how little interest in Roman developments was taken by French architects is revealed by the façade of St Paul-St Louis in Paris of 1634, which once again follows de Brosse's layout. A similar conservatism and innate classicism is felt in the dome and façade of Lemercier's Church of

The interior of the Theatinerkirche, Munich, begun in 1663 by Agostino Barelli. During the construction work he was replaced by the Italo-Swiss architect Enrico Zucalli, and most of the church as seen today is due to the latter. The rich white stucco decorations (executed by Italian workers under G. N. Perti after 1671) are characteristic of the period, despite severe damage suffered in 1944.

The façade and dome of the Theatinerkirche, Munich. The central section of the façade was designed later by François Cuvilliés, the Bavarian Court Architect, between 1730 and 1753.

the Sorbonne in Paris and again in Mansart's and Lemercier's Val-de-Grâce begun in 1645. Nowhere is to be found the dynamism and strong organic unity that is characteristic of the Roman High Baroque, and yet there is the clarity and intellectual precision that give French 17th-century classicism its unique character. The rejection of Bernini's designs for the Louvre in 1665 saw the final triumph of French classicism over the Roman High Baroque, and this is emphasised in J. H. Mansart's Church of Les Invalides (1680–91) and the chapel at Versailles (1689–1710).

The Catholic, Spanish-ruled areas of the Netherlands tended to look to France rather than Italy for inspiration, and the typical French three-storey type of façade was followed in the design of the Jesuit Church in Brussels (J. Francart, begun in 1616 but now destroyed), while the façade of St Pieter in Ghent (begun 1629) is more Italianate in character. The Spanish Netherlands always remained something of a stylistic melting pot and although strong Spanish influence is felt in the extremely ornate top storey of the façade of St Michael in Louvain (designed in 1650), the vault of St Lupus at Namur (begun 1621) instead reflects in carved stone the *ohrmuschel* (ear-shaped) plaster decorations so popular in Germany during the first half of the 17th century. In the mainly Protestant United Provinces of the Netherlands a hybrid style

29

evolved in the hands of architects such as Hendrick de Keyser and Jacob van Campen. The Westkerk in Amsterdam was begun by de Keyser in 1620, but the effect is fundamentally that of a Late Gothic building reworked in an Italian Renaissance idiom. Jacob van Campen's Nieuwe Kerk at Haarlem (1645) with its quasi-central plan is of more interest for its influence on Wren and St Stephen Wallbrook, London (1672–87) than for its Italianate elements. The invasion of the United Provinces by Louis XIV in 1675 ended the Golden Age of Dutch Art and during the 18th century the Netherlands became an artistic backwater.

Throughout the 16th century there was a strong influx of Italian forms and ideas into Germany, Austria and Bohemia, and at the opening of the 17th century the situation in Germany was comparable to that of the Netherlands. However, during the course of the century, an increasingly wide division becomes apparent between Northern and Southern Germany, with Northern Germany looking mainly to the Netherlands for inspiration and Southern Germany looking to Italy. The Michaelskirche in Munich (begun by Friedrich Sustris in 1583) reveals considerable Gothic influence in its planning, but the grasp of Italian principles and the accuracy with which the classical elements are employed in the interior show a far greater sophistication than anything seen in the Netherlands. This is in complete contrast to the slightly later Marienkirche at Wolfenbuttel in Lower Saxony (1604–26), one of the best churches built in Northern Germany during this period, where only the decorative elements show an attempt to break away from the Gothic style.

The tendency in Southern Germany to look to Italy for inspiration was reinforced by the activity there of various Italo-Swiss families of architects and master-builders, from both the Vorarlberg and the Como areas. After the Michaelskirche in Munich the next important step was taken when Archbishop Wolf Dietrich von Raitenau decided to rebuild Salzburg Cathedral. Santino Solari, from Como, began the new cathedral in 1614 after Scamozzi's plans had been rejected, and it was the first purely Italian church to be built north of the Alps. The wide open space of the nave is flanked by chapels and galleries between the buttress piers, and leads to the brightly lit area under the dome. The chancel and transepts are equal, with apsidal ends, while the three-storey façade is flanked by towers echoing Maderno's plans for the façade of St Peter's.

Salzburg Cathedral should have inspired a great many new
churches, but the Thirty Years War (1618–48) so devastated the

Germanic lands that little of any importance was built until the 1660s and a full recovery was not made until the closing decades. There is thus a sharp break in architectural activity of about forty years and when important building projects started again the families of the Italo-Swiss and North Italian architects dominated the field once again. The Theatinerkirche in Munich was begun in 1663 by Agostino Barelli, an architect from Northern Italy, after vain attempts had been made to commission the church from Guarini. Barelli took as his model S. Andrea della Valle in Rome, the mother church of the Theatine Order, and designed an extremely dignified interior with a three-bay nave, apsidal choir and deep transepts, with the crossing area covered by a drum and dome.

Contemporary with the Theatinerkirche in Munich is the façade of the Neun Chöre der Engel-Kirche in Vienna, built in 1662 by Carlo Antonio Carlone for the Jesuits. The church itself has a complicated building history and is fundamentally a Gothic structure, but the ingenious façade, half palace half church, with the central section recessed from the first storey upwards, is strongly Baroque in its *mouvementé* qualities. In the second most important province of the Empire, Bohemia, Carlo Lurago was the most powerful force in Prague during the second half of the 17th century, and held undisputed sway until the arrival of the Frenchman J. B. Mathey in 1675, but the majority of Lurago's work there was for secular buildings.

Lurago's reconstruction of Passau Cathedral (burnt out in 1662) was begun in 1668 and includes several important innovations. The Late Gothic choir was only slightly damaged by the fire and thus dictated the proportions of the remainder of the building. The exceptionally high nave piers are widely spaced and allow extensive views into the spacious side aisles, and the conflict between the classical system of proportions and the structure is very cleverly masked. The second important innovation lies in the use made of a series of shallow saucer vaults, *platzlgewölbe,* to vault the nave, because the use of these on a large scale opened up vast new possibilities for painted decorations. Finally Lurago completely abandoned the ribbed system of the vault of the choir, and the entire central area is decorated with a single large fresco by Carpoforo Tencalla (1678) which leads on to the unified vault decorations of the 18th century.

Carlo Antonio Carlone was also responsible for the abbey churches of Schlierbach (begun 1679) and St Florian (built in

The interior of the monastery of St Florian, built by Carlo Antonio Carlone, 1686–1708. In this church Carlone developed a stage further than at Passau Cathedral the use of a series of platzlgewölbe *to vault the nave. There is no stucco decoration above the heavy entablature and the smoothly plastered vaults are covered with illusionistic frescoes by Melchior Steidl and G. A. Gumpp, 1690–95.*

1686–1708) and the development from Lurago's Passau Cathedral can be seen in them. Both have vaults consisting of a series of *platzlgewölbe*, but while those at Schlierbach are still surrounded by frames of stucco, those of St Florian are smoothly plastered and the entire surface within each bay is painted by Steidl and Gumpp. It only remained for the rigidity of the regular division of the vault into bays to be abolished during the 18th century, and in the last decade of the 17th century the gigantic Late Baroque decorations of the Roman churches by Gaulli, Pozzo and others began to exert their influence.

During the last decade of the 17th century there emerged the first important Baroque architects born north of the Alps and in the first decades of the 18th century the importance of foreign architects was steadily reduced, except in Bavaria and Swabia. In general Baroque architecture (Late Baroque in Italian terms) began to be developed in Austria, and in particular in Salzburg, about a decade earlier than elsewhere in the Germanic lands, while the full Rococo style is hardly found in Austria at all, except in the Tyrol which must be treated artistically as a subdivision of Bavaria. Further, the Rococo style is developed in Bavaria a decade earlier than in either Saxony or Prussia, and the somewhat independent Guarinesque tradition of Baroque architecture is strongest in Bohemia and Franconia. The beginning of these processes is to be seen in the work of Fischer von Erlach and Lukas von Hildebrandt in Austria.

Johann Bernard Fischer (1656–1723), ennobled in 1696, was the son of a Graz sculptor, and left Styria for Italy in (presumably) 1674. He went to Rome and Naples where he worked for 12 years, returning to Austria in 1686, and by 1690 he was firmly established in Vienna. During those 12 years he had made a profound study of Italian architecture at its root sources, instead of through the derivative works of the Italo-Swiss architects, and was profoundly influenced by the dynamism and sculptural handling of masses characteristic of the High Baroque. In addition his activity in Italy coincided with the tremendous outburst of Late Baroque ceiling decorations there, and he rapidly came to understand the possibilities of close co-ordination between architecture and fresco, planned together, instead of fresco decoration applied to a pre-existing, and often much earlier structure.

This union of painting and architecture is fully revealed in Fischer von Erlach's oval Great Hall in Schloss Vranov in Moravia

Opposite, the interior of Passau Cathedral, reconstructed by Carlo Lurago after a disastrous fire in 1662. The very elaborate stucco decorations in the heavy early style were executed by Giovanni Battista Carlone in close co-operation with Lurago.

33

(1690–94), decorated by Johann Michael Rottmayr, and later in the Karlskirche in Vienna. During the 1690s Fischer von Erlach was extremely active in Salzburg in the service of the Prince-Bishop Ernst Count Thun-Hohenstein, who in 1694 commissioned both the little Dreifaltigkeitskirche and the much more important Kollegienkirche. The Dreifaltigkeitskirche develops Borromini's ideas for the façade of S. Agnese in Piazza Navona with a strongly concave central section, while the body of the church is a longitudinal oval with large side chapels on the transverse axis and a deep altar recess. The treatment of the façade is reversed in the Kollegienkirche where the central section strongly protrudes and is held firmly between the crisply modelled flanking towers. Both these churches act as a prelude to the Karlskirche where Fischer von Erlach's sculptural handling of masses is most highly developed.

Fischer von Erlach was succeeded in 1723 as Surveyor General of Imperial Buildings by Lukas von Hildebrandt (1663–1745), whose approach to architecture was very different. The son of a German captain in the Genoese army he was born in Genoa and by 1690 was studying architecture and military engineering in Rome in the studio of Carlo Fontana. He accompanied Prince Eugene on his campaigns in Piedmont in 1695 and 1696 and within

Below left, the abbey of Melk seen from the Danube. Jacob Prandthauer exploited the long, narrow, rocky ledge for his reconstruction of the medieval abbey from 1702. The church nestles between the two long wings of monastic buildings. The courtyard in front exposes the full façade to the river, framed by the magnificent library and 'marmorsaal' which form the ends of the wings. These are treated almost as independent pavilions, articulated with flat pilasters, but they are joined by a low curving gallery pierced in the centre by a large archway which reveals the interior of the church to travellers on the Danube.

Below, the façade of the Kollegienkirche, Salzburg, commissioned in 1694 from Fischer von Erlach. One of the earliest convex façades north of the Alps, it owes a considerable debt to Guarini's palace designs.

a few years he was established as an important architect in Vienna. In contrast to Fischer von Erlach, Rome left less of an impression on Hildebrandt's style than the architecture of Piedmont and Northern Italy in general. His buildings are much less sculptural than Fischer's and the emphasis on lightness and surface decoration characterises the second phase of Austrian Baroque. Hildebrandt was principally a secular architect, but his few churches are important, notably Sv. Vavřinec at Jablonné (Gabel) in Bohemia (begun 1699). The planning of Sv. Vavřinec is an interesting essay in the Guarinesque manner, but the large dome of the central area is orthodox in design with a high drum lit by eight windows. The resemblance between the groundplans of Sv. Vavřinec and the Piaristenkirche in Vienna is so close as to suggest that the latter can be attributed to Hildebrandt although it was completed by other hands, possibly K. I. Dientzenhofer. This church was begun in 1698 and, unlike Sv. Vavřinec, the drum of the dome is omitted so that the dome frescoes come down much lower and the main arches cut into the vault proper. The drum is again omitted from Hildebrandt's Peterskirche in Vienna, which he took over from Gabriele Montani in 1702–07, and drums became increasingly rare in Austrian Baroque churches as the century progressed.

Below left, the abbey of Dürnstein seen across the Danube. This abbey was reconstructed by Prandthauer's cousin, Joseph Munggenast, 1721–25, and stands below the castle where Richard Coeur de Lion was imprisoned. The whole complex is treated in extremely sculptural terms and the tower seems to grow organically out of the platform on which the church is built.

Below, Sv. František, Prague, built by J. B. Mathey, 1679–88. The dry classicism of this Dijon-born architect is in complete contrast to the massive, almost lumpish, forms previously in favour in Bohemia, and it signalled the end of Italian domination in Prague.

Left, the abbey church of Břevnov on the outskirts of Prague, built by Christoph Dientzenhofer, 1708–21. The irregular plan is emphasised by a series of jagged pedimental forms which combine to give the exterior a certain wild vigour.

Below, the vaulting of the pilgrimage church at Křtiny designed by Giovanni Santini in 1710. In this church Santini adopted a relatively orthodox Baroque style, but the interpenetration of the main dome with the four subsidiary domes creates a complicated system of spatial relations in the vaulting.

Jacob Prandthauer was the third great Austrian architect of the generation that includes Fischer von Erlach and Hildebrandt, but unlike them he seems to have been trained as a mason in Austria itself. In 1689 he settled in St Pölten, from where he directed the rebuilding of a series of monasteries including Melk. Prandthauer was very different from Fischer von Erlach and Hildebrandt since he was fundamentally a master-mason and controlled every detail of the execution of his buildings. He never worked for the Court and all his life was spent in the less hectic atmosphere of the great abbeys. Few of his schemes were ever finished completely and from 1701 he directed operations at Sonntagberg, Garsten, St Florian, and Kremsmünster, but above all he is remembered for his reconstruction of the abbey buildings at Melk.

The helms on the towers at Melk were rebuilt by Prandthauer's cousin and superintendent, Joseph Munggenast, in 1738 after a fire. Munggenast was also heavily involved in the rebuilding of the much smaller priory at Dürnstein (1721–25) a few miles further down the Danube from Melk. Here once again the church is aligned at an angle to the river and the view from across the river is all
36 important. The extremely sculptural tower seems to grow organic-

ally out of the platform on which the church is built, and the same rhythmical quality is to be found in the flowing curves of the alternatively convex and concave galleries in the nave.

In 1730–33 Munggenast was responsible for the reconstruction of the monastery at Altenburg near Horn, and the church has one of the richest interiors in Austria. He employed a longitudinal oval plan for the body of the church, with a long choir and altar space, partly derived from Fischer von Erlach and partly from North Italian types, but following Hildebrandt he omitted the drum to the dome. Instead the spaces on the diagonal axes are pierced by large round windows, which light the body of the church, and above rises the splendid apocalyptic fresco by Paul Troger. As at Melk, the pilasters and mouldings are executed in a deep red-brown *scagliola* (imitation marble) while the capitals and other smaller decorative elements are gilt; these act as a foil to the brilliant white sculptures of F. J. Holzinger.

The interior at Altenburg sets the key for the majority of the best Austrian church interiors, but an exception is the abbey church of Wilhering outside Linz (1734–50). There the elaborate and perhaps over-ornate stucco work is Rococo in character and executed by F. J. Holzinger (nave) and the Wessobrun master J. G. Übelherr (transept and chancel). Further, the sculpture is by J. M. Feichtmayr, another Bavarian master, and thus the Bavarian influence is unexpectedly strong.

Bohemian and Moravian architecture was dominated throughout the early 18th century by the Dientzenhofer family. Georg Dientzenhofer was Bavarian by birth, but by 1678 he and his five sons, all architects, had settled in the rapidly expanding city of Prague. The most distinguished members of the family were Christoph with his son Kilian Ignaz, and Johann, all of whom were profoundly influenced by Guarini. Christoph Dientzenhofer followed Guarini's ideas in the nave of Sv. Mikuláš Malá Strana in Prague (1703–11), where the design consists of a series of intersecting ellipses, and again in the monastery church of Břevnov outside Prague (1708–21). The undulating movement of the walls of the nave of Sv. Mikuláš was further developed in the vault where the *platzlgewölbe* were later merged into a continuous rippling surface frescoed by J. L. Kracker (1760–61). The opposite is true of the vault at Břevnov where the individuality of each vault section is emphasised by the frescoes and stuccoes alternately predominating; the resulting vigour is almost brutal in its effect. A similar contrast can be seen

The abbey church of Kladruby in southwest Bohemia restored by Giovanni Santini, 1712–26. The original structure was Romanesque, but Santini rebuilt the vaults with strange abstract patterns of ribbing derived from Bohemian Late Gothic architecture, and the climax is reached in the exotic 'Gothic' High Altar.

between the façade of Sv. Mikuláš with its gentle, almost Borromin-esque play on curved elements, and the exterior of Břevnov where a system of massive façade elements is wrapped round the structure. Simple Ionic pillars and pilasters articulate the exterior and similar elements are arranged so that the sections thrust forward are articulated with very flat pilasters and those that are held back are articulated with heavy columns, which counters the movement created by the structure itself. This irregular plan is emphasised by the series of jagged pedimental forms which break up the skyline, and the whole exterior has a certain wild vigour.

Even less well known than the work of the Dientzenhofers is that of Giovanni Santini (Johann Santin-Aichel), who has been described by Nikolaus Pevsner as the Bohemian Hawksmoor. Santini (1667–1723) belonged to a family of Italian emigrant stone masons who had been established in Prague for several generations, but relatively little is known about his life or training. He is thought to have travelled to England and Holland as well as to Italy, but by the time he took over the restoration of Sedlec in 1703 he was a fully fledged architect. In the following 20 years he was responsible for an astounding number of buildings both in an orthodox Baroque style and in his own special form of Gothicism. His important works were mostly for abbeys and to a certain extent he reflects growing Bohemian national pride, which tended to be identified with the glories of Bohemian Late Gothic architecture. As the abbeys damaged in the Thirty Years War came to need attention abbots increasingly demanded that their Romanesque or Gothic buildings should be restored rather than demolished and replaced by Baroque buildings as in Austria and South Germany. Sedlec is such an instance and the strange system of plaster ribs clearly reflects the influence of Benedikt Ried in Sv. Barbara (1512–47) at Kutná Hora nearby. Santini's restorations at Kladruby (1712–26) have a more exotic note particularly in the wild abandon of the 'Late Gothic' decorative elements in the high altar and transept altars. However, his masterpiece is undoubtedly at Žd'ár in Moravia where he had work in hand from 1706 until his death.

Santini's influence is confined to Bohemia and Moravia but the activity of the Dientzenhofers extended westwards, and the youngest brother, Johann, was responsible for the abbey church of Banz in Northern Bavaria (1710–18). There the design of the nave is a variation on those by Christoph Dientzenhofer in Prague for the pattern of intersecting *platzlgewölbe* is much more spread out and the edges are treated as flat ribs, which are curved in three dimensions. The forms of these ribs change as the observer moves down the church, giving an immensely lively effect to the vault. This type of handling reaches its culmination across the valley in the church of the Vierzehnheiligen by Balthasar Neumann.

Born in 1687 and trained as a civil and military engineer, Balthasar Neumann was the most important Baroque architect to work in Franconia. His activity was closely related to various members of the Schönborn family in the bishoprics of Würzburg and Bamberg, as well as the electorate of Trier and the bishopric of Speyer, and in 1720 he was appointed with Johann Dientzenhofer surveyor of the future episcopal palace at Würzburg. The architecture of the Schönbornkapelle at Würzburg (1723–36) and the chapel at Schloss Werneck (1734–45) reveal Neumann's dynamic handling of space, which belongs firmly to the Baroque tradition. Throughout his career Neumann retained this preference for clearly defined vigorous forms with the decorative elements strictly subordinated to the structure, in contrast to the Rococo architects of Southern Germany.

Neumann came into continual contact with Gothic ideas, and elements such as the apsidal forms to be found in St Paulinus at Trier (begun 1734) and St Peter at Bruchsal (begun 1738) clearly point to this source and are carried on into the Vierzehnheiligen. Probably the most impressive church by Neumann at the close of this period is that at Etwashausen near Kitzingen-am-Main (begun 1741), where there is no decoration whatsoever and the complex interpenetrating spaces and the massive pairs of plain columns give the interior a clarity and precision that foreshadow Neresheim. This interior also emphasises how rarely Neumann was able to obtain the services of decorators sympathetic to his designs, and in this respect none of his churches rises to the heights of the palaces at Würzburg, Brühl or Bruchsal. The Benedictine abbey of Neresheim was Neumann's last important work and the vault was not finished until after his death in 1753. In contrast to the Vierzehnheiligen he was able to evolve fully the scheme of a nave dominated by a central rotunda, and here the dome is carried on pairs of freestanding columns as at Etwashausen. Lightness vies with monumentality, and in this last church there is revealed the growing trend towards classicism, which is also strongly felt in the brilliant frescoes by Martin Knoller (completed 1775).

Different developments had taken place in the south, in Vorarl-

Opposite, the exterior of the 'pilgrimage church on the green hill' at Žd'ár on the Bohemian Moravian border. Santini was active at Žd'ár from 1706 until 1723, but this small church was built 1719–22.

Below, the interior. Santini based the design of the church on a five-pointed star with five additional pentagonal chapels. The church is dedicated to St John Nepomuk, and the stars symbolise the five stars which, according to the legend, appeared above the saint after he had been thrown into the River Moldau.

Left, the church of Etwashausen near Kitzingen-am-Main, begun by Balthasar Neumann in 1741. Pairs of free-standing columns carry the shallow vault of the central space (a scheme later intended for Vierzehnheiligen) but the lack of stuccoes or painted decoration serves to emphasise the cool precision of Neumann's forms.

The abbey church of Neresheim, begun by Balthasar Neumann in 1747 but not finished until 1792. The central rotunda is again supported on pairs of free-standing columns, but on a vastly larger scale than at Etwashausen. Money ran short and the vaults and columns were constructed of wood plastered over.

Far left, the abbey church of Banz, near Coburg, built by Johann Dientzenhofer, 1710–18. The splendid vault is articulated by a series of broad curved ribs, which carry on the upwards movement of the pilasters and lace the structure together. The main spaces are frescoed by M. Steidl.

41

Left, the façade of the abbey church of Einsiedeln. Caspar Moosbrugger began the church in 1719 but after his death Thomas Meyer took over and completed it in 1735. The strongly convex façade is derived from the Kollegienkirche in Salzburg, but the scale is much larger and the vertical elements are handled more emphatically.

berg, Swabia and Switzerland. There the pace was set by a group of closely intermarried families of Vorarlberg architects and craftsmen who had originated in the Bregenzer Wald. These families, notably the Beers, Thumbs and Moosbruggers always worked together and it is often difficult if not impossible to assess the roles of any particular member in the more important commissions. The principal patrons were the Benedictine and Premonstratensian Orders, which were extremely powerful in this region, but in contrast to the princely patrons of Franconia they allowed their architects a much freer hand. With these families emerged a particular type of church design, usually planned with a longitudinal axis, which derives from the traditional German Gothic hall church. In a typical example the main arches down the sides of the nave are carried to the level of the nave vault, and are often divided at about half their height by deep galleries, while the transepts are relatively little emphasised and the choir tends to be slightly narrower than the nave. Externally churches of this type are normally decorated with twin towers.

Opposite, the abbey church of Obermachtal, begun by Michael Thumb in 1686 but later taken over by Franz Beer and completed in 1692. Here the nave is barrel-vaulted with deep wall-pillars and a gallery, and instead of frescoes the vault is decorated with panels of heavy white stucco foliage by the Wessobrunn plasterer, Johann Schmutzer.

Left, the shrine of St Meinrad at Einsiedeln. The westernmost bay of the nave was developed by Caspar Moosbrugger into a great octagonal space with a central cluster of columns comparable in design to an English Gothic chapter house, and part of this octagon provides the convex form of the façade. The stuccoes and frescoes were executed by the Asam brothers in 1724.

Below, the abbey church of Weingarten, begun by Caspar Moosbrugger in 1715. The façade seems to grow out of the roofs of the little town. The design is more taut and the verticality even more pronounced than at Einsiedeln, and the steeply sloping site is used to overpowering effect.

An early example is the Premonstratensian abbey church of Obermachtal (1686–92), which was begun by Michael Thumb, the architect probably responsible for the abbey church at Kempten (1652–66), and later taken over by Franz Beer. Michael Thumb's son Peter, who had married into the Beer family and was one of the architects of St Gallen, was responsible for one of the most beautiful and successful of all Vorarlberg-type churches, that of Birnau on Lake Constance. Franz Beer on Michael Thumb's death in 1690 became one of the leading architects of the group and examples of his work can be seen in the abbey churches of Rheinau (1704–11) and St Urban (1711–15).

Caspar Moosbrugger is more important, and his life work was centred round the abbey of Einsiedeln where he had become a novice in 1682. In 1684 he was called in to advise on the reconstruction of the abbey church at Weingarten, but work was not begun until 1715 and it is difficult to assess his role since his name does not appear anywhere in the surviving building documents. Although there are superficial similarities between the façades of the two abbey churches both share a common source in the Kollegienkirche at Salzburg, and the parallel almost ends there. Both abbey churches have complicated building histories, but Weingarten progressed more quickly and, as well as Moosbrugger, Johann Jakob Herkommer (died 1717), Donato Giuseppe Frisoni, Franz Beer,

Weingarten is one of the great glories of German Baroque architecture and the longest Baroque church in Germany. The nave consists of three bays with curving galleries leading to the crossing surmounted by a high drum and dome in the Italian tradition. The sense of light and spaciousness is emphasised by the superb frescoes of C. D. Asam (from 1717) where the real architecture is continued convincingly in the paintings.

Christian Thumb and Andreas Schreck (a lay-brother and the clerk of works) all had a hand in its planning.

The plan of Einsiedeln is by contrast more complex and reflects its dual purpose as an abbey church and pilgrimage centre. The second function is centred on the site of the cell of St Meinrad (murdered 861) and the great octagon which forms the western-most bay of the nave was built round this pre-existing shrine. Two bays link this octagon with the choir, which was reconstructed by Franz Kraus on the designs of E. Q. Asam in 1746–51, and Moosbrugger had intended that the second bay should be surmounted by a dome on a drum. This scheme was abandoned for reasons of economy, but must be borne in mind when discussing Moosbrugger's contributions to Weingarten. Once again C. D. Asam received the commission for the frescoes (1724) and his brother Egid Quirin for the stuccoes, but the effect has been spoiled by the modern decorations on the walls, which give the interior a fussy and overdecorated effect. The Vorarlberg type continues through the century and a very late example is to be found in the church of Rot-an-der-Rot (1781–86) by Johannes Baptist Laub. Characteristic of its late date the decoration is very restrained indeed and the cool classicism extends to the frescoes by Januarius Zick (1784).

Throughout the preceding account it has been emphasised that the Baroque style, more or less as defined originally in Italy, held

sway over the vast majority of Central Europe, and where Rococo elements of decoration were employed it was strictly in a subordinate role. Only in Southern Germany is a Rococo style of church architecture, as against decoration, to be found. In fact, the area is even more limited than that of secular Rococo architecture since there are no parallels in church architecture to the brilliant Rococo palaces of Protestant Saxony and Prussia. At the beginning of the 18th century Bavaria was dominated by the Italianate Grison architects Zucalli and Viscardi, and the latter was responsible for the extremely influential Mariahilfkirche at Freystadt in the Upper Palatinate (1700–08). There the dome is supported on eight arches, the four on the diagonal axes being slightly narrower and divided by a gallery, while there is no drum to the dome and it is pierced by four large oval windows. Such a scheme suggests the influence of Piedmontese designs and it was to have considerable repercussions outside Bavaria. Georg Bahr used it as the basis of his designs for the now destroyed Frauenkirche in Dresden (1725–43), the only major Baroque church in the Protestant areas of Germany, and the type was developed later by Johann Michael Fischer, who himself came from the Upper Palatinate.

46   During the decade 1685–95 was born the generation of architects

Above left, the abbey church of Rot-an-der-Rot built by the otherwise unknown architect Johannes Baptist Laub in 1781–86. The cool Louis XVI classicism is characteristic of the period, as is the almost total lack of stucco decoration. The frescoes by Januarius Zick (1784) are separated by broad frames, and the integrity of the architecture is unimpaired.

Above, the Mariahilfkirche at Freystadt built by Antonio Viscardi, 1700–08. Smooth ashlar masonry is employed for the dome and the shape is echoed in the forms of the caps on the four small turrets and the lantern.

Right, the Frauenkirche in Dresden built by Georg Bähr, 1725–43, destroyed in 1945. Viscardi's design was totally transformed in this dynamic composition; the dome forms a single flowing shape with the body of the church below. This is in sharp contrast to the crisp forms of the relatively small helms.

47

Left, the church of St John Nepomuk in Munich, built by the Asam brothers as their private chapel, 1733–46. This high narrow church, with a gallery running all round the interior, fully exploits the scenographic possibilities of light and colour as seen at Weltenburg. The worshipper on entering the church immediately looks upwards to the frescoed vault, lit by concealed windows, and to the group of the Trinity over the altar. The 'window' between the altar proper and this group has been reopened recently and the figure of St John Nepomuk is bathed in light from concealed sources, like St George at Weltenburg.

Right, the abbey church of Osterhoven built by Johann Michael Fischer, 1726–40, and decorated by the Asam brothers. Particularly to be noted is the rippling movement created by the convex balconies down the nave and the canted pilasters on the wall-pillars. The spiral columns of the High Altar, recalling Bernini's Baldacchino in St Peter's, are clear illustrations of the Asams' debt to Italy.

which was to transform entirely South German architecture, including the brothers Cosmas Damian Asam (1686–1739) and Egid Quirin Asam (1692–1750), Johann Michael Fischer (1692–1766) and François Cuvilliés (1695–1768). Cuvilliés's ecclesiastical work is very limited and his importance in the field lies mainly in his refinement of the vocabulary of Rococo decorative motifs. However, the Asam brothers were sent to Rome for their training in 1711, Cosmas Damian specialising in painting and Egid Quirin in sculpture, although both were later also to work as architects. They seized upon the scenographic ideas exploited by Bernini, and their approach to architecture was always that of decorators.

On their return to Bavaria the Asams began a series of brilliant ensembles starting with the abbey church at Weltenburg (begun 1718) where architecture, painting and sculpture are combined together inextricably into a theatrical ensemble. Their intention was to make religious experience as intensely real as possible, as in the group of angels bearing the Virgin up to heaven at Rohr (1717–19) while the Apostles around her tomb draw back in amazement. This synthesis of the native German Gothic tradition of realism with the overwhelming theatrical effects of Bernini was to prove hugely successful and a climax is reached in the now sadly damaged

interior of St John Nepomuk in Munich (1733–46), built as their private chapel.

A distinction must be drawn between the basically French inspired style of Rococo decoration favoured by the Bavarian court and exemplified by François Cuvilliés, and the native Bavarian style evolved by the Zimmermann brothers. The Reichen Zimmer in the Residenz at Munich are the earliest full Rococo ensembles in Germany, and were executed by Cuvilliés in the French style in 1730–37, while a climax is reached in the Amalienburg built in the park of the Nymphenburg palace (1734–39) outside Munich, also by Cuvilliés. The extremely rich naturalistic decorative forms are developed a great deal further than in comparable French examples, and these carved and modelled motifs are gilt or silvered in contrast to the white or delicately coloured backgrounds. In the Bavarian style, however, the gilding is confined to the most important motifs and the remainder of the stucco decorations are either left white or polychromed, while the inclusion of elements such as flowers and small animals point towards the native German tradition of realism.

The basic groundplans of Dominikus Zimmermann's churches at Steinhausen (1728–31) and Die Wies (1745–54) are developed from Baroque examples, and it is in the detail design of various elements that the essential characteristics of the change to the Rococo can be distinguished. The sense of dynamic structure so cherished by Baroque architects from Bernini to Neumann is rejected in favour of an insubstantial almost theatrical ensemble where elements such as the columns have a more decorative than structural function. This change in values is reflected in the abstract shapes of the windows, the disruption of the forms of the arches and, at Die Wies, the series of penetrations through the vault of of the choir. Such a wilful manipulation of structural elements is only possible with a very light structure, and these churches are constructed on a system of beams covered with lath and plaster, giving the architect almost complete freedom. Die Wies marks the climax of the Bavarian Rococo and, while the French style is essentially that of the Court, the Bavarian is that of the people.

Churches in which both the architecture and the decoration are Rococo were always relatively rare, and usually it was a case of Rococo decoration applied to a church that was fundamentally Baroque in character. The Asam brothers and Dominikus Zimmermann were first and foremost decorators and their architecture

The interior of the great Benedictine abbey church of Ottobeuren, designed by J. M. Fischer. Although the structure is Baroque, the stucco decoration by Johann Michael Feichtmayr and the frescoes by Johann Jacob Zeiller are Rococo in character and set the tone for the entire interior. 51

reflects their special point of view, but J. M. Fischer was trained as a mason and architect and the magnificent Rococo decorations in many of his later churches were applied to his structures by other specialists under his direction. Johann Michael Fischer was born in 1692, the son of the municipal master-mason of Bunglenfeld, and after experience in Moravia as well as the Upper Palatinate he became a master-mason in Munich in 1722. The groundplan of his early church of St Anna am Lehel in Munich (1729–39), based on a longitudinal oval nave with a transverse oval chancel, can be compared to that of Steinhausen (1728–31), but the dynamic handling of the piers and the framed oval fresco on the vault are fundamentally Baroque. The decoration here, and of several other early churches such as the abbey at Osterhoven (1726–31), was executed by the Asam brothers and again is essentially Baroque in character.

In contrast to most Bavarian architects J. M. Fischer was keenly interested in the exteriors of his churches as well as the interiors, and the facade of Zwiefalten with its soft flowing curves echoes the rippling movement to be found in the interiors at Osterhoven and elsewhere. The success of Zwiefalten led to his receiving the commission to complete the great Benedictine abbey church of Ottobeuren, which had been begun in the 1730s. J. M. Fischer altered the design of the interior by increasing the size and importance of the central piers and emphasised the diagonal axes with additional altars. The rich Rococo plasterwork by Johann Michael Feichtmayr spreads into the frescoes by Johann Jakob Zeiller, illustrating the dissolution of structure that is characteristic of the Rococo.

J. M. Fischer's last important church, that of Rott-am-Inn (1759–63), shows his centralising tendencies developed further. The central irregular octagon dominates the church and the much smaller square entrance and choir spaces are almost insignificant by comparison. The side altars in the octagon vie in size and importance with the high altar, but above all the church is dominated by Matthäus Günther's vast apocalyptic fresco on the main dome. However the effect of Rott-am-Inn is much more static and crisper than Ottobeuren, and the Rococo plasterwork is drastically reduced in quantity. Further, the autonomy of the frescoes is emphasised by the heavy gilt frames around them, indicating that the high point of Rococo decoration has been passed and that the steady progression towards classicism, and churches such as Rot-an-der-Rot and Wiblingen, has begun.

The abbey church of Rott-am-Inn built by Johann Michael Fischer, 1759–63. Here, the overall effect is much cooler and clearer than in his previous churches. The stuccoes are drastically reduced in quantity and mostly confined to the clearly defined cartouches, while the superb sculpture by Ignaz Günther and the frescoes by Matthäus Günther make it one of the finest of all south German interiors.

S. Andrea al Quirinale, Rome

The church of S. Andrea al Quirinale reveals Gianlorenzo Bernini at the peak of his powers executing an important commission for a generous patron. These factors all contribute towards the creation, during the years 1658–70, of one of the masterpieces of the Roman High Baroque. Pope Alexander VII (1655–67) first mooted the idea of building a church for the Jesuit novices, but the actual commission came from Cardinal Pamphili, the nephew of Innocent X. The site on the Via del Quirinale was constricted by existing buildings and this was probably the immediate reason for Bernini's selection of a groundplan based on a transverse oval. The earliest surviving plan, in the Vatican, shows that he was exploring the possibilities of a small church adjoining the Jesuit novitiate set well back from the street and behind a wall. At this stage the design included a rectangular entrance hall separated from the body of the church by two pairs of columns, which were to be echoed by pairs of columns on either side of the entrance to the sanctuary. In the final design the church was set back only slightly from the street and it opened straight out into the shallow forecourt seen today. These plans were approved by Alexander VII on 26 October 1658 and the foundation stone was laid on 1 November.

Bernini's selection of the transverse oval plan raised certain fundamental problems of orientation, as there is a tendency in such a plan for the transverse axis to be more powerful than the longitudinal axis joining the entrance to the altar, with a resulting loss of emphasis on the high altar. Transverse oval plans during the Renaissance were avoided for this reason, and Fornovo's S. Maria dell'Annunziata at Parma is one of the few exceptions. In fact, such a plan was not unfamiliar to Bernini and he himself had

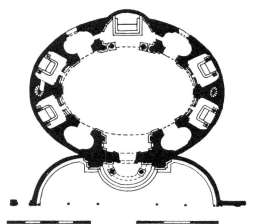

Groundplan of S. Andrea al Quirinale, Rome, built by Gianlorenzo Bernini, 1658–70. The High Altar is placed in the large chapel opposite the entrance and is separated from the congregation space by a partial screen of columns, while the four side-chapels are arranged in pairs on the transverse axis.

0   50 FEET 0   15 MTRS

The complex aedicule motif which separates the High Altar from the congregational space. Bernini cut away the centre of the semicircular pediment in order to frame the white stucco figure of St Andrew passing up to heaven.

The arrangement of side chapels and entrances separated by pilasters. Any tendency for the larger, transverse axis to predominate is controlled by the placing there of a pilaster instead of a side chapel. The upward movement of these pilasters is continued in the ribs of the dome, resulting in a very tightly knit spatial unit. 55

Above, the vault with a system of panelled ribs superimposed upon the hexagonal coffering. Antonio Raggi's white stucco decorations, executed 1662–65, form a brilliant contrast to the gilding. Groups of putti are placed over the smaller windows and pairs of reclining fishermen decorate the larger windows over the side chapels.

Left, the lantern, in effect a miniature drum and dome. From the dove, symbolising heaven, winged cherubs' heads cascade down to form a ring round the 'entrance to heaven'. These in turn are linked colouristically with the white stucco figures decorating the windows.

already used one in his church in the old Palazzo di Propaganda Fide (1634), which was later replaced by Borromini. An influential forerunner is provided by Francesco da Volterra's S. Giacomo degli Incurabili, where the cornice of the longitudinal oval nave is carried round the walls of the sanctuary and the entrance bay. Unfortunately this results in a breakdown of the centrally planned space and a conflict between it and the strong longitudinal axis. Bernini solved these problems in S. Andrea and so gave the structure far greater dynamism than any of its predecessors.

The problem of the transverse axis was sidestepped by Bernini by organising the side chapels so that the axis intersects the oval at a flat pilaster and not on the axis of a side chapel with its subsidiary points of interest. Further, this lack of accent is emphasised by the relatively pale colour of the pilasters compared to the rich red mottled marble of the remainder of the church. The entablature is continuous round the interior of the church until the entrance to the sanctuary is reached, where it breaks forward and forms part of the pediment of an aedicule motif carried by pairs of Corinthian columns. This aedicule motif performs a critical function in the church since the columns act both as a screen, which separates the sanctuary from the congregation, and as a continuation of the oval. The centre of the pediment is cut away and encloses the flying white stucco figure of St Andrew, which is both thematically and spatially the focal point of the structure.

Corinthian pilasters, identical in design to those in the body of the church, are used to articulate the interior of the sanctuary. But while this creates an element of continuity between the two spaces, the pilasters in the sanctuary are cut from the mottled red marble instead of pale marble so creating an atmosphere of additional richness and emphasising its special role. The sanctuary and congregation space are also linked by a pale marble string course, which passes behind the sanctuary pilasters and altarpiece. This string course forms the top moulding of the doors on each side of the aedicule motif and also the capitals from which the arches of the side chapels spring: inside each side chapel it is extended round the interior and is colouristically linked with the pediments over the altarpieces. Further emphasis is also given to the sanctuary by the relatively strong lighting from its small cupola, which contrasts with the mysterious darkness of the empty doorways to each side of the aedicule motif and the dimly lit side altars. Colour and directed lighting are key elements in the dynamic balance.

The main altarpiece, painted by the French artist Guillaume Courtois, depicts the martyrdom of St Andrew and the richly coloured marble frame appears to be borne up by a flurry of angels and putti who cascade from the cupola above. The direction of the real lighting is reinforced by the gilt rays extending downwards (as in the Cornaro Chapel of 1645–52) and these appear to pass behind the painting. Further rays radiate out in all directions from the ring below the cupola, and pass into white stucco clouds, heightening the illusion.

Turning from the spatial linkage of the two spaces to their thematic connections, it can be seen that the altarpiece and the figure of St Andrew represent the same action on two different spiritual levels. His martyrdom takes place in the altarpiece, where the angels clustered round holding the martyr's palm and crown of roses witness the steadfastness of his faith, while the white stucco figure in the congregation space represents his spirit passing up to heaven. On the vault of the cupola surmounting the main dome is painted the dove, symbolising heaven, and further cherubs' heads line the ring and cascade from above. Thus the entire interior of the church is dedicated to the sacred mystery of the martyrdom of St Andrew and the worshipper is a witness of this mystery. Such illusionistic ensembles were developed during the Renaissance and in particular by Raphael in the Chigi Chapel, but Bernini gave these ideas greater coherence and made the illusion more explicit.

The articulation of the congregation space is as subtle and complex as that of the sanctuary, for all the most powerful movements lead to the figure of St Andrew. Further, the extension of the action of the altarpiece into the congregation space, in the form of the figure of St Andrew, solves the problem inherent in centrally planned spaces, of directing attention towards any point outside that space. The saint is framed within the pediment of the aedicule motif. On entering, the observer's eye is inexorably carried, by the massive plain entablature sweeping round the interior, towards the climax of the pediment. This entablature also acts as the division between the richly coloured marbles of the earthly zone of the church and the white and gold of the heavenly zone of the dome.

Bernini's design for the dome is a revealing contrast to that of S. Tomaso di Villanova at Castelgandolfo, for he rejected the classical distinction between drum and dome proper and amalgam-
58 ated the two, almost in the manner of 15th-century umbrella

Above, two of Raggi's white stucco fishermen.

Below, the Martyrdom of St Andrew over the High Altar. Guided by the gesture of the angel, St Andrew gazes up to heaven, here located in the small cupola above, and the source of lighting for the painting is located there also in order to create a coherent illusion.

domes. As at S. Tomaso, he superimposed a system of broad ribs over classical coffering (a device first evolved by Pietro da Cortona at Ss. Martina e Luca), but these are irregularly spaced so that they continue the organisation of the chapels. Further, the omission of a drum enabled Bernini to carry the ribs down to the entablature and to create a strong visual link with the pale marble pilasters below. Thus the upward movement of the pilasters of the body of the church is carried on by the ribs and directed back down to the pilasters on the opposite side. This creates a strongly dynamic space, and for the observer entering the church the focus of this web of forces is the figure of St Andrew.

Bernini also used directed light to the same end in the congregation space and creates a powerful positive/negative relationship between the aedicule motif and the entrance, for while the entablature breaks forward at the aedicule motif, it is recessed into the window embrasure above the entrance. Indeed, the semicircular window above the entrance may be considered the negative of the semicircular pediment of the aedicule motif and through this element the organisation is carried to the outside of the building. This window is much the largest in the church and since it is opposite St Andrew, it is his strongest source of light, while the variation in sizes of the other windows is hardly noticeable.

The white stucco figures over the windows are linked by a continuous looped garland, like that at S. Tomaso, and this is carried right round the interior of the church, adding further richness to the window zone and softening the terminations of the ribs. Over the larger windows pairs of male figures with the paraphernalia of fishermen are the symbolical companions of St Andrew, while groups of three putti gambol over each of the smaller windows. These putti had great influence on the Asam brothers and the motif of the putto using a garland as a swing occurs repeatedly in their decorations. The stucco work was carried out by Antonio Raggi between 1662 and 1665, and parts of the decoration were not completed until 1670. The altarpieces for the side altars were even more delayed and Gaulli's *Death of St Francis Xavier* was not painted until 1706, though these are of relatively minor importance.

Bernini's treatment of the exterior of S. Andrea may again be compared to S. Giacomo degli Incurabili, where large scrolls also transfer the thrust of a dome encased in a cylindrical structure. The mass of the heavy parapet enables the thrust of the dome of S. Andrea to be absorbed within the structure of the side chapels

Above, St Andrew carried up to heaven after his martyrdom. In the lower zone of the church, the saint is portrayed in life-like colours, but above the entablature the heavenly world predominates and the colour scheme is instead white and gold.

Below, the decoration of the small vault over one of the side altars, continuing the themes found in the main vault.

Left, the vault over the High Altar with Bernini's brilliant illusionistic ensemble. The altarpiece with its heavy marble frame seems to be carried by the flurry of angels and putti which tumble out of the cupola above.

Below, the façade of S. Andrea al Quirinale based on two aedicule motifs, one inside the other.

Right, in the hands of Bernini colour became an extremely important part of the design, both in a symbolic role, distinguishing the earthly from the heavenly zone, and as a unifying element. To draw attention to the aedicule motif, and the High Altar beyond, the pairs of Corinthian columns are cut from a rich red and white mottled marble in contrast to the pale marble used for the pilasters.

without any further buttressing, and the strongly plastic treatment of this parapet is carried on into the façade. A shallow conical roof leads to a cupola, but these are only visible from a distance.

The position of the church set back from the street means that the observer comes upon it suddenly and first sees it from relatively close quarters. Bernini designed a strongly plastic façade with these sharp oblique views in mind. The façade proper consists of a double aedicule motif, the larger continuing and developing the mouldings of the parapet while enclosing the smaller, which develops the mouldings of the casing enclosing the side chapels. Further, the rigid jutting forms of the triangular pediment of the larger motif, developed from his façade of S. Bibiana, find their foil in the much richer and more sculptural forms of the portico. The semicircular arch within the larger motif defines the window and in doing so links the façade with the aedicule motif framing the sanctuary inside. This link between the interior and the exterior is developed one stage further by the curved walls framing the forecourt, since these lead the eye instinctively towards the central doorway and act as a foretaste of the spatial organisation to be found within.

Early sketches by Bernini have revealed him experimenting with the idea of replacing the cupola with a gigantic cross of St Andrew, and this would have meant that the final expression of the mystery revealed inside was to be seen in symbolic form on the exterior of the building. However, the present state of the building both inside and out is that intended by Bernini, except that the level of the forecourt has been lowered, leading to a distortion in the proportions of the curved walls and an increase in the number of steps from three to ten. This alteration has appreciably damaged the very subtle proportions of the façade. Nevertheless S. Andrea al Quirinale remains Bernini's masterpiece.

S. Ivo della Sapienza, Rome

The association between Francesco Borromini and the authorities of the Archiginnasio in Rome began in 1632 on the recommendation of Bernini, and his earliest work was concerned with the completion of the south range of the building. This rather austere structure, which was later to become the seat of Rome University, was begun by Giacomo della Porta at the behest of Sixtus V, and there fell to Borromini, in 1642, the task of inserting the new church into the pre-existing courtyard. Thus Borromini was not only faced with the problem of an extremely cramped site, but also with the necessity of designing a structure whose exterior would harmonise with the dry Counter Reformation style of Giacomo della Porta. It is indeed a tribute to Borromini's skill and ingenuity that he succeeded on both counts and still created one of the masterpieces of the High Baroque in Rome.

In the introduction emphasis has been laid on Borromini's rejection of the classical anthropomorphic system of planning in favour of a non-anthropomorphic system based on angular relationships like that favoured by Gothic architects. Such a system was employed by him in S. Carlo alle Quattro Fontane, completed except for the façade in 1641, and at S. Ivo the ground-plan is again based on triangles. This time the equilateral triangles have a common centre and form in basis a regular six-pointed star. Six-fold symmetry was extremely rare in Italy before 1600, and Vitozzi's SS. Trinita at Turin, begun in 1598, is perhaps the only surviving example. But Borromini is much more likely to have arrived at this basic plan by experimenting with mathematical forms than by other influences. The groundplan here is further complicated by developing alternate points of the star into simple

Above right, the interior looking towards the High Altar. The underlying basic design is not easily comprehended and the immense variety provided by the different designs for the short sections of wall adds to the complexity, but the heavy entablature weaving its course round the interior stabilises the design.

Below right, a section through S. Ivo showing the construction of the vault and finial (from Opera del caval. Francesco Boromino . . . , 1720*). Borromini intended the niche containing the High Altar to be flat-topped, but later it proved necessary to insert an arch in order to stabilise the structure.*

VIII

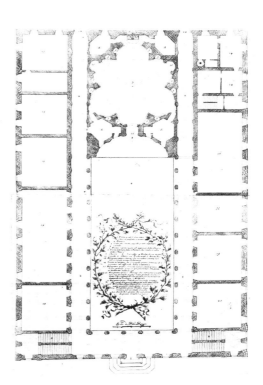

The engraved groundplan of the Archiginnasio,
Rome, later the seat of Rome University and now
of the State Archives. The two long wings
flanking the arcaded courtyard were designed by
Giacomo della Porta, together with the
hemicycle which closes it opposite the main
entrance. Francesco Borromini inserted the
church of S. Ivo into the space behind the
hemicycle, using a six-pointed star as the basis
of his design.

semicircular forms and closing the others at half their depth by convex forms. This means that convex and concave walls alternate with short straight sections, creating an immensely plastic boundary to the interior space of the church.

Borromini disregarded the problems raised by the transverse axis and instead laid heavy emphasis on the series of giant pilasters that articulate the whole interior of the church. These pilasters, by their very regularity, impose a discipline and order, but the system is further complicated by the series of niches between them. Every recess comprises a large niche flanked by two smaller niches, so producing a system of triads. Further, all the smaller niches are very similar in design, so creating a new rhythm. The resulting ambiguity in the grouping of elements is comparable to that in S. Carlo alle Quattro Fontane, but here the system is greatly refined and two further rhythms are introduced by the two string courses, since that passing round the church at two-thirds the height of the pilasters is interrupted by the altar niche, while that passing round the level of the capitals is interrupted by the convex sections. All these devices contribute towards the dynamic restlessness of the space, although the effect has been temporarily muted by the 19th-century painted marbling on the walls.

The complexity of the walls is temporarily resolved in the heavy entablature which runs uninterrupted around the interior of the church, and this emphasises with great clarity the basic groundplan. But above this level Borromini developed an entirely new type of dome. Instead of employing a transitional zone, as in S. Carlo, the complex groundplan is extended upwards until by gentle softening the complexity is resolved into a simple circular ring on which is set the cupola. The vault is divided into six bays and the system of triads seen below is maintained, but as the eye travels upwards the difference between adjoining bays steadily diminishes until the cherubs' heads are reached. The long bands of stars serve to emphasise the continuity and, although different designs alternate, the windows are close in spirit. Such a vaulting system again has Gothic overtones, though no direct parallels can be drawn with specific Gothic buildings. The colour scheme of the dome is white and gold (as was originally the whole church with the exception of the pilasters), and when the current restoration is completed the interior will once again be seen in its former purity and simplicity.

Throughout his work Borromini shows a passion for symbolism and S. Ivo is no exception; the six-pointed star is itself the symbol

Opposite, the interior of the dome. Borromini's designs for architectural elements, such as windows, always reveal an immense inventiveness, and the broken pediments and other features here show the bizarre juxtapositions of forms for which he is famous.

Left, the High Altar. Pietro da Cortona received the commission for the complicated altarpiece (depicting S. Ivo as the lawyer of the poor with Christ appearing to a group of saints, including S. Ivo above) but it was unfinished at his death in 1666, and was not completed until many years later.

Right, a detail of the vault showing how the complex groundplan revealed by the entablature is gradually resolved and softened until the perfect circle below the lantern is reached. The white and gold decoration of the vault is original, while the marbling is the result of later redecorations.

of wisdom (*sapienza*). The twelve niches in the lowermost zone, according to Borromini himself, symbolise the twelve apostles; the same significance is attached to the twelve stars round the ring of the cupola, while the tiny vault of the cupola itself reveals a sunburst probably representing God as the centre of the Universe. Such ideas were fully developed in Borromini's reconstruction of the nave of S. Giovanni in Laterano, where the undersides of the arches are decorated with palm trunks, a motif derived from the descriptions of the Temple of Solomon. Palm trees were originally intended by Borromini to rise from the tops of the windows in S. Ivo, but these were replaced by emblems of the Chigi Pope Alexander VII. His coat of arms conveniently includes eight-pointed stars, so the two different patterns of stars are scattered freely all over the interior of the church. They are worked into the Corinthian capitals of the pilasters and also between alternate modilions in the cornice.

66   Pope Alexander VII commissioned the altarpiece from Pietro da

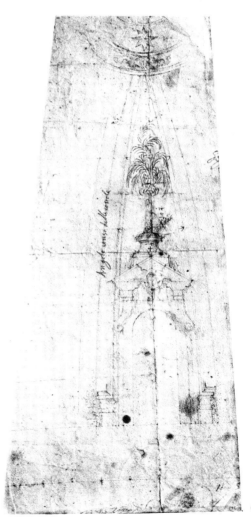

Below, Borromini's drawing for the proposed decoration of one panel of the vault of S. Ivo, now preserved in the Albertina, Vienna. The palm tree is a reference to the Temple of Solomon, but in the church this was rejected, and instead the vault was decorated with emblems of the Chigi Pope, Alexander VII.

Cortona, probably in 1661, but it was left incomplete at the painter's death in 1666. It was apparently still incomplete in 1674 and it was eventually finished by Giovanni Ventura Borghesi da Città di Castello from the master's designs. However the lower section depicting S. Ivo as the lawyer of the poor is considerably inferior to the upper section representing, as if on a tapestry, Christ appearing to a group of saints including S. Ivo. The subject matter is thus closely tied to the dedication of the church but no thematic links comparable to those of S. Andrea al Quirinale were possible here.

The exterior of S. Ivo presents almost as many surprises as the interior, since the structure becomes more and more eccentric as the eye travels up it. The lowermost two storeys are basically the hemicycle built by Giacomo della Porta well before Borromini took over. Borromini's main task was to fill in the arcade, leaving only relatively small windows to light the hexagonal sacristies that occupy the spaces between the hemicycle and the church interior. The structure of the church itself is very light, and to stabilise the structure and absorb the thrusts of the dome, Borromini had to consolidate the otherwise flimsy structure of the hemicycle. In fact the area between the last bays of the hemicycle and the long arcades are heavily reinforced to act as buttresses to the church, and the structure was not finally stabilised until the northern range was completed by Borromini with the construction of the Biblioteca

Alessandrina in the north-east corner. The hemicycle received an attic storey and the buttresses were capped with gigantic Chigi Monte, which have the double function of providing weight for the buttress system and of masking the area of contact between the top floors of the ranges and the casing of the dome.

In the design of this casing, Borromini's genius begins to emerge in the rhythmic sequence of units, which echo the organisation within. The sexfoil plan of the casing is subtly exploited for its dynamic possibilities, and this is most clearly seen in Borromini's use of pilasters. Single pilasters articulate the bowed surfaces of the sexfoil while massed pilasters articulate the re-entrant angles, and this gives the effect of swelling forms restrained by the stronger pilasters. This sense of restraint is emphasised by the curved buttresses, which lead up to the cupola while the stepped roof continues the bowed forms of the sexfoil below. But these buttresses are not merely decorative; they coincide with the re-entrant angles of the groundplan within and are the main structural units carrying the weight of the cupola and dome down through the body of the church. The finials have exactly the same function as those on Gothic flying buttresses—that of controlling the side thrust and directing it downwards. Apart from these main structural units, the remainder of the dome consists of thin infilling to lighten the structure. A delightfully witty touch, wholly characteristic of Borromini, is provided by the crisply carved moulding forming part of the entablature. Here the normal classical moulding has been replaced by one composed of putti heads flanked by pairs of wings.

The design of the cupola reveals Borromini's continued pre-occupation with structural problems, as well as giving him an opportunity for demonstrating his taste for the bizarre. Basically the design for the lower section develops that of the cupola over the dome of S. Carlo, with its vigorously modelled re-entrant curves in the entablature, while the columns are doubled to give greater monumentality. Inside the cupola single columns occupy the angles of the hexagonal lantern, and these, combined with the pairs of columns outside, are the load-bearing members, which carry the weight of Borromini's spiral crowning motif and transfer it to the buttress system. It has been suggested that Borromini gained inspiration for the re-entrant curves in the lantern entablature from exotic classical sources, and certainly similar forms were known at Baalbeck (engraved by Belon, 1555) and at Tivoli

The exterior of S. Ivo seen from the courtyard designed by Giacomo della Porta. Borromini reinforced the hemicycle and added an attic storey in order to absorb the thrust from the dome behind. The swelling forms of the drum enclosing the main vault are continued in a series of curved steps leading up to the lantern, and this immensely dynamic composition reaches its climax in the bizarre spiral finial. Most of the structure was complete by 1650.

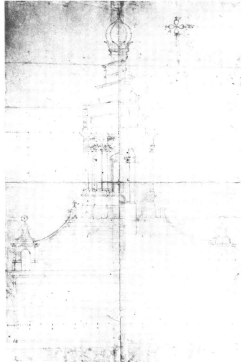

Above, Borromini's design for the finial of
S. Ivo, now preserved in the Albertina, Vienna.

Left, the dome and finial of S. Ivo seen over the
roofs of Rome. The ascending spiral motif has
a long history stretching back to the
architecture of ancient Babylon, but
Borromini's interests were probably as much
mathematical as archaeological.

Right, the campanile of S. Andrea delle Fratte,
Rome, built by Borromini, 1653–65. The exotic
finial, partly made of metal and supported by a
series of caryatids with folded wings, is a
characteristic exercise in pure fancy and to a
certain extent developed from S. Ivo.

(a tomb now vanished). Such sources were common in the 17th century and a notable example of their influence is the façade of Rainaldi's S. Maria in Campitelli. However, the spiral motif presents special problems and suggested sources range from Babylonian ziggurats to rather more lowly sea shells, of which specimens were in Borromini's possession at his death. The closest parallel is provided by a print of 1572 by Martin van Heemskerk representing Babylon, but the surviving drawings show that Borromini conceived the structure as a pillar supporting the crown finial, encircled by an ascending spiral motif, suggesting that the genesis was more mathematical than archaeological.

Borromini exploited similar forms again for his tower of S. Andrea delle Fratte (1653–65), but there the pairs of columns on the lantern are replaced by pairs of caryatids with long folded wings and the entablature is even more broken up. However, the extraordinary structure of inverted volutes carrying a crown, this time of metal, is an exercise in pure fancy and a worthy successor of the finial of S. Ivo. Borromini unfortunately was compelled to abandon work on S. Andrea delle Fratte before he had completed the dome, but the dome is again cased in a drum as at S. Ivo and the lessons learnt there about dynamic handling of such surfaces if taken a stage further. Buttress forms are projected outwards to create an almost square structure with four façades and, while the centre of each façade echoes the outward curve of the dome within, it is controlled by deep concave curves to each side. He intended to crown this remarkable structure with a lantern whose concave forms would have created a dynamic balance in opposition to the convex forms below, following the same reversed relationship between the convex and concave forms of the drum and lantern of S. Ivo.

It is hardly surprising that Borromini's ideas received little support in Rome, although their influence north of the Alps was to prove incalculable, and they remained little understood before the arrival of Guarino Guarini. Bernini respected Borromini as a superb technician and engineer, not his own strongest point, but his bizarre caprices profoundly disturbed him. Bernini is recorded as having described Borromini as an eccentric whose architecture was extravagant, for while other architects based their proportions on the human body, Borromini based his on fantasy. He concluded, somewhat bitterly, that in his view it was better to be a bad Catholic than a good heretic.

S. Agnese in Piazza Navona, Rome

Following his election as Pope Innocent X in September 1641, Giovanni Battista Pamphili decided to reorganise the Piazza Navona, which had grown up on the site of the Circus of Domitian. This had been traditionally identified as the scene of the martyrdom of St Agnes and, as far back as the 8th century, a shrine had existed there to commemorate her death. A diagram of the old church, drawn by Pompeo Ugonio and now in the Vatican Library, shows that the church was aligned in the opposite direction to that of the existing building and that the entrance was in the Via dell'Anima, then known as the Via Mellina or the Via di S. Agnese. The old structure had been built as a parish church in 1419, but in 1581 it was handed over to the Congregazione dei Chierici Regolari Minori (the Caracciolini), in whose possession it remained until 1652, by which time it was totally inadequate for their needs.

It is unlikely that the pope's interest in the church was due to anything more than its close proximity to his family palace and his desire to make the Piazza Navona the grandest in Rome. However, he stated his intention to be buried in the church, and this alone called for its rebuilding on a rich and splendid scale. Prince Camillo Pamphili was placed in charge of the operations and the foundation stone was laid by Camillo's son on 15 August 1652. The architects selected were the aged Girolamo Rainaldi and his son Carlo, both of whom were currently working on the Palazzo Pamphili. As in almost all Roman churches, the immediate problem was the constricted site. This was relatively shallow and the Pamphili naturally desired as large a church as possible; so, discounting any eccentric relationship between the façade and the interior, a centrally planned structure was the only solution. The

The façade of S. Agnese in Piazza Navona, Rome, with Bernini's Fountain of the Four Rivers in the foreground. To the left of the church lies part of the Palazzo Doria-Pamphili and to the right the Collegio Innocenziano, altogether an incomparable Baroque ensemble.

73

Above, Girolamo and Carlo Rainaldi's design for S. Agnese of 1652, now preserved in the Albertina, Vienna. The unusually high attic storey and the drumless dome combine to give the design a somewhat heavy, squat effect.

Left, Francesco Borromini's first design for S. Agnese (1635). Before the decision was taken to allow the façade to include part of the palaces to each side, the site was too narrow to allow fully developed flanking towers. However, in this design the turrets are given considerably greater prominence, and they contribute to the strong verticality obtained by the addition of a high drum to the dome.

Rainaldis reorientated the church, so that the main façade was now in the Piazza Navona, and they adopted a Greek cross plan with the short arms terminated by straight walls. Further, the piers of the crossing were intended to present broad surfaces on the diagonal axes and these were to contain chapels in the form of deep niches framed by pairs of columns. The articulation of the central area would then have been based on an irregular octagon with alternate large and small arches.

Between the interior of the church proper and the façade a vestibule was planned, and this was to have led out on to an impressive flight of steps into the piazza. However, the façade itself was to be flat, with three large doors, and the exceptionally high attic storey was to be crowned with two low towers. The towers may have been intended as bases for two large statues, and other statues were certainly planned for the balustrade. Finally behind these there was meant to be a relatively low dome, without a drum, giving the church a somewhat heavy, squat appearance.

Work on the church began briskly enough. The travertine was quarried at Tivoli, or removed from the Forum, while white marble for the sculpture was transported from Carrara, but despite this promising start progress was soon interrupted. The Rainaldis were criticised because the steps leading up to the entrance extended too far into the piazza and after only a year they were dismissed by the pope. Prince Camillo was also dismissed following his quarrel with his domineering mother, Donna Olimpia, who was furious that he had married the Principessa di Rossano, widow of Paolo Borghese. Donna Olimpia herself would have given the commission to Bernini, but Innocent X instead chose Borromini to complete the building, and he took over in August 1653.

By this time part of the façade had been built and the piers of the crossing were standing up to the height of the niches. This severely limited Borromini's alterations, but one of his first acts was to demolish the central section of the façade. He abandoned the vestibule and by doing so he was able to set back the central section of the façade and join it to the end bays by strongly concave units. The new scheme with the concave façade was shown on a medal struck in 1653. Here, although the very narrow end bays are retained, Borromini has abolished the high attic storey and given the small cupolas considerably more character. Further, he has planned a much higher dome with a drum and a large lantern crowned by a characteristically exotic motif. The great projecting

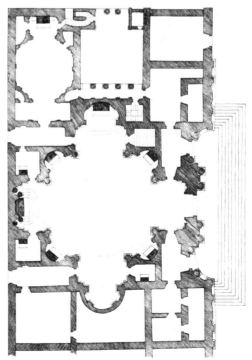

The groundplan of S. Agnese as built (from J. J. de Rubeis, Insignium Romae Templorum prospectus, 1684). *After the purchase of the Palazzo Ornano in 1653, Borromini was able not only to enlarge the façade but also to add a large sacristy and courtyard to the design. The broad flight of steps leads down into the Piazza Navona while the wall behind the High Altar adjoins the Via dell'Anima.*

Left, the façade from across the Piazza Navona. Basically the design of the façade, up to the level of the entablature, and that of the drum to the dome are by Borromini, while Carlo Rainaldi was responsible for the reintroduction of the high attic storey and the small pediment over the main entrance. Borromini's designs for the flanking towers were also altered drastically by Rainaldi.

flight of steps is abolished while the Rainaldis' system of three large doors is retained.

Borromini's plans for the interior were also heavily restricted by the work already completed, and in his first project he retained a doorway, at the end of the left-hand arm, leading into the courtyard of the adjoining Pamphili palace. (He probably intended to balance this with a small funerary chapel for the pope, leading out of the right-hand arm.) In addition, the eight red *Cottanello* marble columns articulating the crossing piers in this project were intended to be well sunk into recesses prepared for them close to the niches. Later Borromini made further alterations to the plans and again changed the character of the interior, providing the basis for the design of the church as seen today. He filled in the recesses prepared for the large marble columns and instead moved them into the space of the four main arches of the crossing. This in effect reduced the width of these arches while increasing the width of the piers, and the gaps between the columns and the niches were filled with full pilasters in white marble. The colouristic balance is such that the red columns are the strongest elements and they give the effect of a regular octagonal space with different developments on alternate sides. Finally, he settled for apsidal endings for the two side arms

Right, the High Altar with the white marble relief of the Holy Family with Angels by Domenico Guidi, which was completed between 1674 and 1686. The rich colours of the marbles, green and red, give the interior a sombre magnificence, while the white marble altarpieces gleam like jewels.

76

and made these into additional side chapels by abandoning the doors. The high altar, entrance bay and major side chapels include a great deal of *verde antico* marble, and this rich but sombre material emphasises the depth of the arms. But the red and white marble of the central area, bathed in light from the dome, are in strong contrast and enable the central space to dominate the composition.

Borromini's first intentions for the design of the façade were also drastically revised since, late in 1653, the Pamphili succeeded in purchasing the Palazzo Ornano adjoining the church on the opposite side to the Palazzo Pamphili. After the old palazzo was demolished, Borromini used part of the space for a large sacristy flanked by a courtyard; the rest of the site was used for the Collegio Innocenziano, including the famous Pamphili Library. These changes were relatively unimportant, however, compared to the new possibilities made available for the façade. Borromini increased its width to include part of the palaces to each side; he also doubled up the paired pilasters of the end bays designed by the Rainaldis and inserted between them a convex wall section ornamented with a complex aedicule motif to act as the lowermost storey of a pair of flanking towers. Unfortunately, the details of these towers were by no means executed entirely according to Borromini's intentions.

Innocent X urged the work on and by his death in January 1655 the entrance bay had been vaulted and the façade had risen to the height of the entablature, while work was proceeding on the drum and dome. Donna Olimpia then took charge of the building and the new pope, Alexander VII, sent her a warning to press on with the work and clear the piazza, which was cluttered with building materials. Soon afterwards she left Rome and once again handed over the responsibility for the work to her son Dom Camillo. However, difficulties arose between him and Borromini and progress slowed down, until finally Borromini abandoned the commission. In 1657 Carlo Rainaldi was again appointed architect and, with the assistance of Giovanni Maria Baratta and Antonio del Grande, the church was finished. During this last phase, Rainaldi made efforts to alter the design wherever the building was incomplete. He reintroduced a high attic storey to the façade and substituted the present, rather insignificant triangular pediment for the complex double pediment planned by Borromini. The attic storey conceals the plain lower section of the structure of the dome and completely alters the dynamic balance between the various parts of the building, since Borromini had intended the long low

B.C.—4

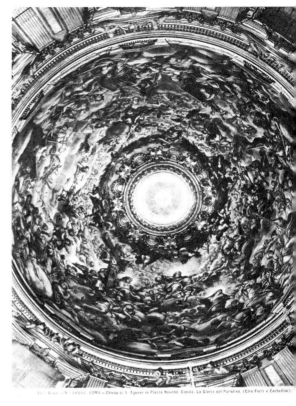

Above, the dome frescoed with the scene of the Virgin welcoming St Agnes into heaven. This was commissioned from Cirro Ferri in 1670 but at his death in 1689 the work was still dragging on and Sebastiano Corbinelli did not complete the fresco until the end of the century.

Left, the side altar dedicated to St Emerenziana. She was the foster-sister of St Agnes and according to the legend she was stoned to death two days after St Agnes's martyrdom whilst praying beside her grave. This accounts for the prominence given to an otherwise very obscure saint.

79

façade to be in strong contrast to the pronounced verticality of the dome and towers, while the point where these opposing forces met was to be articulated by the extremely sculptural pediment. Further, Rainaldi weakened the vertical accent in the lantern by reducing the number of columns from sixteen to eight, and convex forms are employed throughout the height of the towers instead of the concave forms intended by Borromini for the top storey, which were to be in dynamic contrast to the forms below.

The vertical emphasis in the interior of the church is perhaps even stronger, though again the influence of Rainaldi and his collaborators is considerable. The *Cottanello* columns provide vigorous vertical elements and their role is emphasised by the unusually forceful handling of the entablature above them. This breaks forward to form separate architectural elements, which both continue the upwards movement of the columns and close off the side arms from the octagonal central space. A further unusual feature is the use of subsidiary elements or attics above the entablature. These act as pedestals from which the vaults spring, enabling additional height to be gained without distorting their semicircular form. These attics are omitted from the pendentives and as a result these have unusually tall proportions. Borromini's elegant drum and dome form the climax of this strong upward movement, and the pointed form of the latter marks the finale of the long series of Roman dome designs originating with Giacomo della Porta's revision of Michelangelo's dome for St Peter's.

Innocent X intended that the interior of the church should be one of the most sumptuous in Rome, and instead of painted altarpieces he commissioned from Alessandro Algardi a series of seven large-scale marble reliefs. Algardi had evolved this new genre in St Peter's with his gigantic *Meeting of Leo and Attila* (1646–53), and by his death in June 1654 he had only started work on the relief of the *Martyrdom of St Agnes* and the bronze statue of the pope intended for his sepulchral monument. Although the church was dedicated in January 1672, the decoration was carried on until well into the 18th century and the high altar relief depicting the Holy Family by Domenico Guidi was not completed until 1724. Undoubtedly the two finest reliefs are the *Death of St Cecilia* by Antonio Raggi (1660–67) and the *Stoning of St Emerenziana*, begun by Ercole Ferrata in 1660 and finished by Leonardo Reti after his death (1689–1709). The two reliefs intended for the altars in the side arms were abandoned in favour of single figures, the

St Agnes on the pyre, carved in white marble by Ercole Ferrata in 1660. The saint is represented at the dramatic climax, when the power of her prayer has rendered her immune to the fire. However, compared with Bernini the draperies are relatively restrained and closely tied to the structure beneath, showing the impact of Algardi's classicism.

very dull St Sebastian by Pier Paolo Campi (completed 1719) and Ferrata's brilliant *St Agnes on the Pyre*. The flying draperies of the latter and the painterly treatment of the flames point to the influence of Bernini, but otherwise the figure owes more to the realist classicism of Algardi than to the intense spirituality of Bernini.

The painted decoration of the church is confined to the pendentives and dome, while the remainder of the vaults are decorated with bands of rich white and gilt stucco ornament. Giovanni Battista Gaulli painted the four large pendentives with allegories of the four virtues, but once again there were considerable delays. He had been introduced to Camillo Pamphili by Bernini and had received the commission in 1666, but the frescoes were not executed until 1672. The brilliant colours and luminosity are in complete harmony with the richness of the interior below, while the frescoes of the dome appear by comparison thin and monotonous. These were commissioned from Pietro da Cortona's assistant Cirro Ferri in 1670, but at his death in 1689 the work still had not been completed and they were finished by Sebastiano Corbellini at the end of the century. The scheme is derived from Pietro da Cortona's dome of S. Maria in Vallicella of 1647–51, with much greater prominence given to the gilt stuccoes round the base of the lantern. These are intimately connected with the large wreath born by putti, while heavenly light pours out from a source behind, which is identified with the dove on the vault of the lantern.

It may be asked where the importance of S. Agnese lies since so many different architects and artists were involved in its construction and decoration, and so little was completed exactly as they had intended. Even so, in many ways the church must be considered as a conscious High Baroque revision of the plans for St Peter's. Here the problem of the interrelationship between the dome and the façade are solved, and the elegant and yet dynamic dome is in perfect harmony with the towers. Inside the church the central octagon dominates and yet complements the side arms, while the main piers with their vertical emphasis are a clear reworking of those of St Peter's. The rich sculptural decoration forms a museum of Roman Baroque sculpture, and the series of altar reliefs afforded a constant source of inspiration for Late Baroque designs, including Juvarra's Superga. S. Agnese is probably the greatest example of Baroque church decoration in Rome and with Bernini's Fountain of the Four Rivers they together provide an incomparable Baroque ensemble dominating the Piazza Navona.

The Martyrdom of St Emerenziana. The modello for this marble relief was submitted by Ercole Ferrata to Camillo Pamphili in 1660, but it was unfinished at the sculptor's death in 1686. In 1689 the commission was entrusted to Leonardo Reti who finally completed it in 1709, but not without extensive alterations to Ferrata's design in the top left-hand area.

S. Maria della Salute, Venice

One of the most interesting and exciting of all Italian Baroque churches outside Rome is that of S. Maria della Salute in Venice, begun by Baldassare Longhena in 1631. In the previous year Venice had been struck by a particularly severe outbreak of the plague, and the Republic decided to erect a church dedicated to the Virgin as an offering for the deliverance of the city. S. Maria della Salute carries the double meaning of health and salvation, and the dedication draws attention to the dual role of the Virgin. Three senators were appointed to select a site and recommend an architect. They chose an area close to the Dogana on the island between the Canale della Giudecca and the Grand Canal, near the point where the two merge into the Canale di S. Marco. To make room for the new church it was necessary to demolish the Seminary of the Somaschi, and a new seminary was built later by Longhena (1669) adjoining the church. The senators held a competition to select the architect and 11 projects were submitted in early April 1631, by which time the site had already been cleared and the foundation stone laid.

Three important specifications were included in the conditions of the competition; first, on entering the church the worshipper should be able to take in the whole space with an unobstructed view. Secondly, bright light should be evenly distributed throughout the interior, and, thirdly, the view from the entrance should be dominated by the high altar and as it is approached the side altars should come into view. Further, the new church had to be suitably grand, fit in with its surroundings, and not cost too much (60,000 ducats). Out of the 11 projects submitted those of Baldassare

Longhena and of Antonio Fracao and Zambattista Rubertini

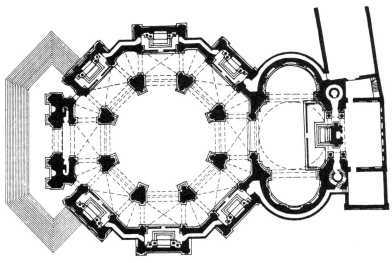

Above, a general view of S. Maria della Salute from across the Grand Canal. To the left lies the Dogana, or Customs House, and between this and the church the Seminary rebuilt by Baldassare Longhena in 1669.

Left, the groundplan of S. Maria della Salute, showing the main octagon leading into the presbytery with semicircular apsidal spaces at each end. Longhena placed the High Altar within the archway which separates the presbytery from the choir.

0   100 FEET   0   30 METRES

83

Left, the central octagon seen from the main entrance. As stipulated in the competition rules, only the High Altar is clearly visible on entering the church, and it is not until the worshipper reaches the centre of the octagon that the six side altars come into view.

were chosen for further consideration, but the committee experienced great difficulty in reaching a final decision, and, even after it had been increased by three, the decision was referred back to the full Senate which voted in favour of Longhena.

The Fracao/Rubertini scheme envisaged a longitudinally planned church, but Longhena submitted a much more subtle modified centrally planned structure whose domes would dominate that side of the Grand Canal. Baldassare Longhena (1598–1682) began as a sculptor, trained under his father, but when he turned to architecture he studied under Vincenzo Scamozzi, who in turn was the most influential pupil of Palladio. He thus belongs to the great tradition of architects in the Veneto including Palladio, Sansovino and Sanmicheli, and echoes of these Renaissance masters are seen in his buildings. The model Longhena submitted is now lost but the accompanying memorandum survives and gives a certain amount of information about his earliest intentions. He chose with God's blessing, a circular form for his church in the shape of the Virgin's Crown, and he took care to stress the originality of his proposals. This crown is an allusion to the Queen of Heaven, whose help was implored in the Venetian Litany recited by processions at times of plague, and figures of the Virgin occupy the most important positions on both the high altar and the exterior of the church.

Longhena's model was basically the same as the church in its final form, but the proportions were altered; in particular the presbytery was increased in size. The choir was reduced, and the width of the aisle round the main octagon was also increased. Further, the clarity and logic of the entire building is greatly enhanced in its final form and Longhena clearly refined the design
considerably between the submission of the model in 1631 and work

The High Altar with sculpture by Giusto le Corti, 1670. The Virgin as Queen of Heaven dominates the structure and intercedes on behalf of the suppliant figure of Venice, while a haggard female figure representing the plague is driven out by a putto. This iconography emphasises the role of the church as a votive offering to the Virgin, the protector of Venice, for the deliverance of the city from the plague of 1630.

starting after the foundations were laid September-November 1633. His choice of a modified centrally planned design probably stems partly from the specifications stipulated in the competition, and partly from a synthesis of Palladio's longitudinal church designs with the modified centrally planned designs of Early Baroque architects active in Northern Italy, though the inspiration for such a design can be traced back through Bramante to Brunelleschi. However one of the most important effects of the greater significance given to the presbytery was the increase in size of the dome vaulting it. This in turn reduced the dominance of the main dome, and with the addition of the pair of high campanili a rich and harmonious ensemble was created.

Centrally planned churches with side aisles were rare in the Renaissance, but this type of building was relatively common in late Antiquity, and the church of S. Vitale at Ravenna (completed 547) provides an illuminating comparison, particularly in the design of the piers supporting the dome. In S. Maria della Salute, these piers are articulated by large attached columns on high pedestals, as used by Palladio, and they thrust forward reinforcing the centrality of the octagon. The flat dados in effect give the central space an irregular 16-sided form, which is further emphasised by the small sections of the balustrade set forward above the cornice. At this point an additional novelty is seen because the columns are not carried on into the drum, but instead support heavy pedestals on which are placed eight large wooden figures of prophets.

The 16 round-headed windows of the drum are arranged in pairs, separated by broad flat pilasters supporting the upper balustrade; above rises the ribbed and coffered dome maintaining the sixteenfold symmetry. Longhena's design for the piers of the octagon was absolutely crucial for the success of the interior, because of the multiple functions they were required to perform. Apart from the entrance bay and the bay leading into the presbytery, the side walls of the aisle are extended outwards to provide six side chapels, which instead of being the full width of the sides of the octagon, are the same width as the arches of the central octagon. This meant that Longhena could design the main piers so that the inner surfaces of the arches were exactly repeated in the entrances to the side chapels and again with half-pilasters beside the altarpieces. Further, the entablature above the pilasters on these main piers is repeated in the aisles and side chapels as a continuous moulding and extends

Above, a side altar. Longhena extended the side walls of the aisle round the octagon to provide six side chapels, and these were designed the same width as the arches of the central octagon. The same order articulates the insides of these arches as the side chapels themselves, thus creating a series of coherent spaces.

The pavement of the octagon. Here Longhena used the pavement skilfully to centralise the composition and emphasise the symmetry. The outermost portion of the design takes up the octagonal form of the inner space and the central area resolves these complexities into a progressively simpler circular design. As a subsidiary effect, the design also encourages the visitor to stand in the correct spot to appreciate fully the views into the side chapels.

into the presbytery. The axes of the side chapels are given greater force by several other devices, and the aisles are broken up into sections by the half-columns on the piers and on the entrances to the side chapels, while the sections of aisle leading into the side chapels have high quadripartite vaults, the kite-shaped sections between have simple lower vaults. Light too plays its part and the segmental windows in the side chapels, derived from Palladio, allow more light to pour into the central area. Consequently there is a strong sense of organic unity between the central octagon, the aisles, and the side chapels and this is carefully developed and maintained both in the rest of the interior and on the exterior of the church.

The presbytery is only loosely connected with the body of the church, and unlike the schemes of Borromini and Guarini there is no interpenetration of spaces, but a great sense of continuity is created by Longhena's use of the orders. As has been explained, the central octagon is articulated with a giant order of attached Corinthian columns while the aisles, side chapels and subsidiary faces of the piers are articulated with a smaller order of Corinthian pilasters and half-columns. In the presbytery this smaller order is used for the entrance arch and again as full columns in the screen framing the high altar that divides the presbytery from the choir, but for the deep apsidal forms to each side of the central space, Longhena returned to the giant order of the octagon. The entrances to these apsidal forms are framed with half-columns while pilasters on the same scale separate the two storeys of windows. The pedestals are replaced by a continuous low panelling beneath these pilasters, and while the entablature carried by these pilasters is at the same level as that carried by the giant order in the octagon, the entablature of the smaller order reappears as the moulding separating

the two storeys of windows. These two spaces are thus extremely subtly interrelated and the system with modifications is carried on into the choir behind the high altar. There the giant pilasters are abandoned, but with minor modifications the two-storey system of the presbytery is carried on and the storeys are each articulated with small pilasters.

In accordance with the specifications, the high altar dominates the church and this unusual freestanding structure is topped by a lively group of the Virgin as Queen of Heaven, by Giusto le Corti, with a suppliant Venice kneeling to her right and opposite a haggard woman, representing the plague, is driven out by a putto. Originally the south wall of the choir was pierced with a window so that the head of the Virgin was bathed in a bright light, but now the soft general lighting all comes from the windows of the presbytery and the figures tend to be silhouetted against the relative darkness of the choir. The group is supported by caryatids in the form of angels while in the centre, under a cover, is the Byzantine image of the Virgin, which was one of the relics brought from the church of S. Tito in Crete by Francesco Morosini in 1672. To each side are figures of S. Lorenzo Giustiniani and St Mark completing the complex. Further sculptural decoration is included in the spandrels of the arches of the presbytery and above the high altar recline the Evangelists John and Mark.

Longhena's scenic approach to planning, with vistas across spaces, is developed from that of Palladio and is in complete opposition to the dynamic spatial effects created by Bernini and most other Roman architects. On entering the church only the high altar is seen, as if through a series of arches, and the remainder of the spatial organisation remains mysteriously out of sight until the worshipper moves down the longitudinal axis towards the high altar. Then the carefully integrated views into the side chapels are discovered and finally the apsidal forms of the presbytery. This is in complete contrast to S. Andrea al Quirinale, where the whole structure is revealed on entering the church. Instead of the eye passing from plane to plane, as if through a series of theatrical wings, it follows the walls and dome where all elements inexorably converge on to the figure of St Andrew enclosed in the pediment. The absence of this tendency for the eye to move along the forms in S. Maria della Salute reveals a fundamental difference between the dynamic effects of the Roman High Baroque and the scenographic effects of the Venetian High Baroque. The connection

The richly picturesque exterior of S. Maria della Salute without which the Grand Canal is now unthinkable. Only two of the outside walls of the side chapels are visible from the Grand Canal and these are treated as small independent church façades, while the entrance is given particular emphasis by the triumphal arch motif articulated with giant Corinthian columns.

between Longhena and the theatre can be further elaborated, for not only does the scenery overlap but the floor also rises with the perspective. Longhena adopts this device in S. Maria della Salute, where the presbytery is approached by three steps and the choir is set one step higher again—a feature not found in Roman High Baroque churches. Further, the progressive diminution in size of the orders and the windows as the choir is reached also points to this source of inspiration and increases the sense of recession.

Palladio is the source of Longhena's use of the colouristic contrast between grey stone and whitewash, which was a medieval technique taken over and refined by Brunelleschi. In the Florentine tradition the whitewash was used to differentiate the filling from the grey stone of the structural elements. This system was rejected by the Roman High Baroque architects, but Longhena used the contrasts for pictorial purposes though he abandoned the logical approach of the Florentines. For example, the unity of the central octagonal space is emphasised by the huge grey stone columns placed in front of whitewashed piers, while in the presbytery the system is reversed and the pilasters are whitewashed with the spaces between them grey. Indeed the dome is handled even more pictorially since the 16 ribs are light brown in colour and the same colour is employed for the pilasters of the drum. These are contrasted with the grey window surrounds, but their bases of grey stone establish their connection with the giant order below.

The exterior of the church is extremely rich and picturesque, both in the interrelationship between the domes and campanili and in the wealth of sculpture. The main dome is constructed with an inner and an outer shell separated by a system of beams and the false lantern of the inner dome is lit from the base of the external one. This outer shell is supported on a low plain drum, which acts as a transitional zone between the octagonal drum and the curved surface of the dome, while the smaller dome follows the Venetian-Byzantine tradition with its stilted form over a simple circular brick drum. Here Longhena again followed Palladio, who had employed such a dome framed by campanili for the church of Il Redentore in Venice. However the most striking elements in the composition are the splendid scrolls, which link the octagonal drum to the larger octagon of the aisles. These scrolls have an important structural function since they act as buttresses taking the weight of the dome and spreading it out. S. Maria della Salute is built, like all Venice, on piles and it is impossible to load any

The cluster of domes and campanili dominating the Grand Canal. The most striking elements in this composition are the huge scrolls which, apart from their decorative function, serve to spread the weight of the dome. This ensures that if the church sinks into the soft ground on which Venice is built, the sinking will be uniform and will not endanger the stability of the structure.

Left, the exterior of the octagon seen from inside the courtyard of the Seminary. Those side chapels not visible from the Grand Canal were left almost undecorated by Longhena, but their relationship to the outside of the aisle surrounding the octagon is clearer here than on the front of the church.

Below, a detail of the great decorative scrolls and their sculptural decoration. The infilling of the scrolls is panelled with coloured marble, but several centuries of weathering has left this almost as pale as the white marble of which the rest of the church is constructed.

point too heavily without the risk of sinking. To stabilise the structure Longhena designed the side chapels and façade so that they act as abutments for the dome; the scrolls provide the structural continuity between them.

In the lower zone the exterior walls of the chapels to the left and the right of the central façade are both visible from the Grand Canal and are treated as small church façades in their own right. The lower halves are articulated with four pilasters between which are shallow niches containing sculpture, while the attic is pierced by a semicircular window and crowned with a pediment and more sculpture. Such a system is reminiscent of Palladio's Chiesa delle Zitelle and the debt to Palladio is even more explicit in the main façade. Here Longhena gave particular importance to the entrance wall by using a triumphal arch of giant columns on high pedestals while the subsidiary order, from which springs the arch, continues 92 the order used in the exterior walls of the chapels. Further, the giant order is exactly that used inside to articulate the octagon; similarly the smaller order corresponds to that articulating the aisles and the chapels. The niches containing statues in two tiers between the giant columns follow the proportions of the presbytery windows, while the scale and general layout of the entrance arch is repeated again by the arch leading into the presbytery and a third time in modified form by the arch enclosing the high altar.

Such homogeneity between the interiors and exteriors of churches is rare in Rome, though Pietro da Corona's Ss. Martina e Luca is an example. Nowhere else is the perspective vista extended so forcibly to the exterior of the church, and the effect is analogous to the *frons scenae* of the Renaissance theatre where perspective vistas are seen through the openings. S. Maria della Salute became very influential when, at the close of the 17th century, many architects turned from Rome to Northern Italy in search of the scenographic values characteristic of so much Late Baroque architecture. Buildings such as Carlo Rainaldi's Jesuit Church at Loyola, St Mary at Gostyn in Poland by Pompeo Ferrari and even Gibbs's Radcliffe Camera at Oxford owe a great debt to Longhena; explicit, if curious, homage is also provided by the rotunda of the Tate Gallery in London.

Andrea Palladio's designs for the Frons Scenae *of the Teatro Olimpico at Vicenza. Designs such as these probably suggested to Longhena the scenographic ideas he included in the planning of S. Maria della Salute.*

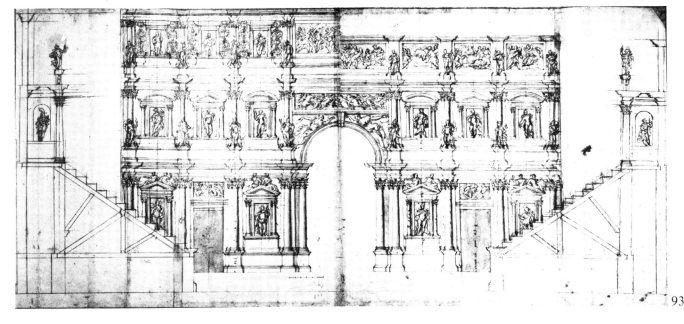

Guarino Guarini in Turin

S. Lorenzo and the Cappella della SS. Sindone, which lie adjacent to the Royal Palace in Turin, are Guarino Guarini's only surviving major ecclesiastical works. These extremely exciting structures reveal a highly individual style, which is totally divorced from orthodox Roman High Baroque architecture, and indeed far beyond anything planned by Borromini. As mentioned earlier, although so little of his architecture is still standing, his work and designs are extremely well documented by his architectural treatise, of which the engravings were published in 1686 under the title of *Dissegni d'archittetura civile e ecclesiastica*. Later the architect Vittone edited the unfinished text and this was published with the engravings in 1737. These engravings were the vehicle by which Guarini's ideas were spread to the areas north of the Alps (for relatively few architects would have had the opportunity of studying many of his buildings); they were also one of the starting points for the tremendous flowering of Baroque architecture in Central Europe, particularly in Bohemia, Moravia and Franconia.

Guarino Guarini was born in Modena in 1624 and at the age of 15 he entered the Theatine Order, which sent him to Rome for his training. There he studied in the monastery of S. Silvestro al Quirinale and, apart from theology, acquired a considerable knowledge of philosophy, mathematics and architecture. In addition, he had the opportunity of studying first-hand the latest developments in Roman High Baroque architecture and clearly the work of Borromini was the most sympathetic to him. In a sense Guarini was to be the natural successor to Borromini, particularly in his adoption of a non-anthropomorphic system of architecture and in his interest in interlocking spaces. But while Borromini

The view into the main dome of S. Lorenzo in Turin, designed by Guarino Guarini, 1668–87. In Guarini's designs the solid structure of the dome, familiar from Roman Baroque architecture, is replaced by a diaphanous system of ribs, and the thin infilling between these is either pierced with windows or omitted altogether. This photograph was made after the removal of later decorative painting.

always maintained a continuous regular movement round his spaces, creating an organic unity, Guarini's architecture is full of contradictions and surprises. The well-developed scenographic qualities in Guarini's churches link him with the traditions of Northern Italy. The continuity of the Gothic tradition there may also be said to be a common factor he shares with Borromini, for they both approached the problems of architectural planning from a geometrical standpoint.

In 1649 Guarini returned to Modena and assisted Father Castiglione, also a mathematician, in the construction of S. Vincenzo there and the adjoining Theatine monastery. However in 1660 he settled in Messina, where he taught philosophy and mathematics and first practised architecture independently. The façade of his church of the Annunziata was destroyed in the earthquake of 1908, while his plans for the church of the Padre Somaschi (although illustrated in his treatise) were never carried out. Two years later he had to return to Modena on the death of his mother, and from there he was sent to Paris to build the Theatine church of St Anne-la-Royale. Guarini returned to Italy to work on the Theatine church in Turin, S. Lorenzo, before the completion of his work in Paris and St Anne-la-Royale was heavily modified before it was completed in 1720. Thus by the time Guarini settled in Turin in 1666 he was a mature and well-established architect; S. Lorenzo marks the beginning of the most brilliant period of his activity, although neither in this church nor in the SS. Sindone did he have an entirely free hand from the start.

S. Lorenzo had been begun in 1634, but its construction was suspended soon afterwards, and although in 1668 Guarini had to take over an already started building, the structure of the church as seen today is entirely due to him. The original plan for the church provided for an octagonal main space with shallow side altar recesses and a separate sanctuary, probably rectangular with apsidal ends. This was a typical North Italian type of church design, of which another familiar example is S. Maria della Salute in Venice (begun 1634), but in the hands of Guarini the design was transformed beyond recognition. By 1679 the structural work was complete, and the architect himself celebrated the first mass.

The main space is treated as a centrally planned area, and the perimeter is defined by a series of concave forms on the diagonal and transverse axes and the entrance bay, while a large arch opens into the sanctuary. However a new perimeter is established in

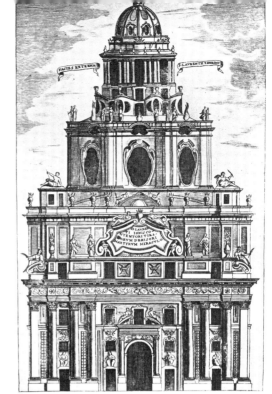

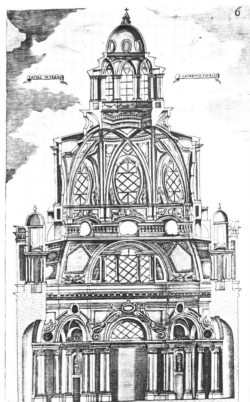

6

the zone above the main order where there are gently convex forms on the longitudinal and transverse axes and strongly convex forms, bevelled below the pendentives, on the diagonal axes. This new perimeter is supported by the 16 red marble columns, which are free-standing within the body of the church and carry an entablature that breaks back to the outer perimeter at each arch. In effect, all eight sides of the octagon are formed of enormous convex Palladian motifs, but while the entrance bay and lateral axes have very shallow niches, the diagonal axes have small chapels. This contributes additional spatial ambiguity to the scheme by making the outer perimeter almost square. Palladian motifs are also used for the

Opposite and below, the exterior as planned, the section through the main dome, and the groundplan of S. Lorenzo in Turin–all engravings from Guarini's Dissegni d'architettura civile e ecclesiastica *of 1686. These engravings illustrate well the complex spatial planning, zone by zone, adopted by Guarini, and the interpenetration between the main space and the altar space.*

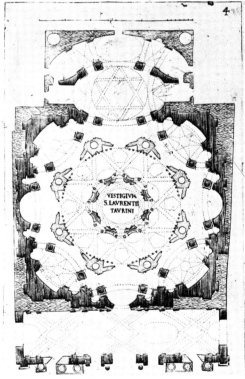

Left, a side altar, S. Lorenzo. The complex relationship between the outer perimeter and the vaults above seems almost wilful, but Guarini's precision has been obscured by later decoration. 97

windows on the main axes, but there they are doubled, the front motif acting as a screen, separated from the window by a lenticular space.

Guarini redesigned the sanctuary so that the space was oval, with the high altar in the centre and another arch leading into the curved choir behind. This sanctuary is treated as an independent centrally planned space except that its convex curve provides the form of the side of the main octagon; so, by implication, the two spaces interpenetrate. The vault here is relatively simple with the drumless 'dome' divided into a series of panels by six broad ribs forming a six-pointed star, the lower part pierced by six large windows. However the lighting in the sanctuary is relatively low compared to that of the main space, and there is no lantern to the dome. This is in complete contrast to the complexity of the main dome above the pendentive zone, where the solid structure of the classical type is replaced by a diaphanous structure of ribs and windows.

Below left, a vault in the Great Mosque at Cordova in Spain, completed in 975.

Below, vault of the church of S. Miguel del Almazan, Spain, 13th century. The sources of Guarini's dome designs remain conjectural, but he clearly knew about early Spanish designs as he mentioned the Talvera Chapel in the old cathedral of Salamanca in his treatise. Such building techniques remained in use in Spain until the middle of the 16th century.

98

The exterior of S. Lorenzo as built. The façade designed by Guarini was never built and instead the church was engulfed by one wing of the Royal Palace. This photograph is taken from the main courtyard of the palace.

The ring of the dome is pierced by eight kidney-shaped windows, with pediments above, and these reintroduce eightfold symmetry for the higher zones of the dome. In the first zone a network of eight ribs spans the space, three units at a time, leaving a central octagonal space leading to the higher zones; the lower part of this zone is pierced by eight oval windows with pentagonal openings above. Otherwise the spaces between the ribs are, where possible, left open and lit from concealed windows. Borromini frequently designed vaults employing systems of ribs, but he never dispensed with the infilling between the ribs in the way which Guarini developed. The second zone of the dome repeats the structure below, but with the ribs spanning the space two units at a time and with the omission of any other penetrations, while in the topmost zone, the complexity is further reduced and a simple octagonal dome is pierced by eight small windows.

'Vaults', said Guarini, 'are the principal parts of architecture', and throughout Guarini's centrally planned churches the vaults

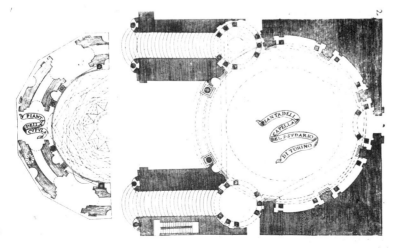

Above left, the staircase giving access to the
Cappella delia SS. Sindone from the south aisle
of Turin Cathedral. Guarini ingeniously solved
the problem of alignment between the stairs and
the chapel by inserting triangular vestibules at
the top.

Above and left, section and groundplan of the
Cappella delia SS. Sindone, engraved in
Guarini's treatise. The problems of the dual
function of the chapel were solved in principle by
Amadeo di Castellamonte when he chose a
ninefold symmetry for the interior, but it was left
for Guarini to exploit fully the possibilities this
most unusual scheme afforded.

became so complex that they totally dominate the structure. The connection with the ribbed vaults of Borromini has already been indicated, but additional, if not more important, sources were probably the Hispano-Moresque ribbed vaults in buildings such as the Great Mosque at Cordova (finished in 975) and the later vault of the church of S. Miguel de Almazan at Soria. Unfortunately Guarini does not appear ever to have written the section on vaults for his treatise, and the influence of these buildings must remain conjectural. Elsewhere in the treatise, however, he analysed the difference between classical and Gothic architecture with particular reference to their respective vaulting systems, and he was clearly sympathetic to such exotic sources. The interior of S. Lorenzo was highly decorated, contrary to the intentions of Guarini, but following damage during the war, the majority has been taken away, and now the main dome is seen as Guarini would have wished, although strictly the pendentive paintings should also be removed. The façade of the church was never built and from the piazza Guarini's two-tiered dome appears to rise out of an undistinguished secular building, although the external structure of the dome closely follows its internal organisation.

The Cappella della SS. Sindone was under construction at the same time as S. Lorenzo, and again Guarini took over an unfinished structure. One of the holiest relics, the Holy Shroud, was owned by the House of Savoy, and this had been transferred from Chambéry to Turin by Duke Emanuele Filiberto in 1563. Plans for a new church to house it were eventually abandoned in favour of a scheme for a large chapel to be built between the choir of the old cathedral and the Royal Palace. Since it was also intended as a sepulchral chapel for the House of Savoy, the original inspiration was probably provided by the Cappella dei Principi in Florence (begun 1603). The chapel was to be built at the level of the piano nobile of the palace, and thus be easily accessible from the state apartments as well as from the body of the cathedral itself, at a considerably lower level.

In 1655 Carlo Emanuele II gave the commission to Amadeo di Castellamonte (who died in 1683) and by the time that Guarini took over in 1667, the structure had been built to the level of the cornice. The original plan provided for a simple cylindrical structure articulated by giant pilasters with Palladian motifs between, probably to be vaulted with a plain spherical dome, and joined to the cathedral by a large arch leading into the choir above the high

A detail of one of the bronze capitals which crown the giant pilasters. Characteristic of Guarini's fertile genius for inventing new decorative motifs, this is based on a normal Corinthian capital, but worked into the design are the crown of thorns and the nails of the Passion.

101

altar. Access from the cathedral is gained from the transepts by flights of stairs rising alongside the choir, so as to allow pilgrims to circulate freely, while a third entrance on the main axis connects with the palace. Guarini inserted three circular vestibules at these entry points and in doing so entirely altered the character of the structure. Further, the vestibules at the heads of the stairs are articulated with three sets of three columns, which most ingeniously solve the difficult problems of alignment between the stairs and the chapel. Amadeo di Castellamonte had designed the chapel with a ninefold symmetry so that a double bay linked up with the cathedral and a single bay with the palace; the triangular symmetry of the vestibules is continued by Guarini in the pendentive zone of the chapel.

Pendentives are perhaps the wrong word for these curious structures, since the bays between the vestibules are joined by broad arches running over the curved surface of this zone and these link the round body of the chapel with the round ring of the dome. Their lack of function is further emphasised by the fact that they are pierced by oval windows very similar to those over the vestibules, and these are directly over the pilasters, which have no structural function whatsoever. The body of the chapel is executed in black marble and there is little ornament except for the superb black bronze capitals of the giant pilasters, which include the instruments of the Passion. This sombre richness is more pronounced in the pendentive zone where the dark grey stone is carved with intricate patterns of stars and crosses, again reminiscent of Moorish architecture.

With the windows in the pendentive zone Guarini established the six-fold symmetry of the upper zones of the dome, and the purpose of this pendentive or transitional zone becomes clear. In it the nine-fold symmetry of the pilasters of the body of the chapel is reduced to the three-fold symmetry of the arches and then increased in the windows to the six-fold symmetry needed above. The lowermost zone of the dome is relatively orthodox with six round topped windows separated by broad piers with somewhat Borrominesque aedicule motifs, while a more eccentric note is struck by the deep window embrasures, which are treated as short barrel vaults with honeycomb coffering. Above this rises an extraordinary cone-shaped structure consisting of successive zones of segmental arches, each springing from the centres of the arches below, and these are divided vertically by console motifs with windows to each side.

The interior of the dome. In the pendentive zone, the ninefold symmetry of the body of the chapel gives way to a threefold symmetry, and above the circular ring the dome structure proper is based on a sixfold symmetry. However, the intricate patterns of stars and crosses, with which the surfaces of the pendentive zone are carved, again suggest the influence of Moorish architecture.

Thus this portion of the dome consists of a diaphanous structure of 36 arches and 72 windows, and an additional element is created by the mouldings of the arches rising from each junction, which provide 12 zig-zag shapes snaking upwards. The console motifs form part of the system of twelve buttresses, which carry the weight of the dome and the principles involved can be compared to those employed in the dome of S. Ivo della Sapienza. But, as in S. Lorenzo, Guarini has taken the decisive step of replacing the infilling between the ribs by windows. The central area of the vault is covered by a shallow saucer dome with concealed lighting from twelve small windows, but silhouetted against this is a ring-shaped structure forming a 12-pointed star, which in turn acts as a frame for the dove in the sunburst on the centre of the surface of the saucer dome —the focal point of the composition. This star effectively forms a cut-off dome so that the space above is flooded with a strong, celestial light in contrast to the dark grey stone below, while the recessive effects of the tiers of arches makes the interior of the dome seem much higher than in fact it is.

Of the exterior of the Cappella della SS. Sindone only the dome can be easily seen, and even this rises up out of the jumble of the Renaissance cathedral and the surrounding secular buildings with little relationship to them. So Guarini treated it entirely independently and instead of the plastered surfaces of S. Lorenzo, great use is made of sharply cut brick. The round-headed windows of the drum are united by the undulating cornice, and above this level 12 buttresses ornamented with urns run up to support the cupola and crowning motif, while the structure of the inside of the dome is closely mirrored on the outside. Guarini appears to have intended a Borrominesque spiral motif to crown the dome, and the curious structure with three tiers of small oval windows is something of an anticlimax. The chapel was completed in 1690, seven years after Guarini's death, but the interior, in contrast to S. Lorenzo, faithfully reflects his intentions, with the exception of the white Neo-Classical tombs of the House of Savoy, which strike an alien note. The ingenuity and forceful handling of these brilliant dome structures makes the loss of Guarini's longitudinal churches the more regrettable, but the domes have exerted an almost magical fascination on architects ranging from those of the late 17th century to Nervi, and the ideas exploited in them are vital for any understanding of certain trends in Baroque architecture in Piedmont and north of the Alps during the 18th century.

The exterior of Turin Cathedral with the dome of the Cappella della SS. Sindone. Guarini's masterpiece dominates the Quattrocento cathedral but is entirely buried between it and the Royal Palace, and so seems to float among the roofs. Unfortunately, Guarini's spiral finial was rejected in favour of the present curious structure, which is something of an anticlimax.

103

The Karlskirche, Vienna

Fischer von Erlach's Karlskirche in Vienna provides an interesting parallel to S. Maria della Salute in Venice, for both were founded as votive churches after attacks of the plague. The Emperor Charles VI fulfilled his vow of 1713 to St Charles Borromeo for the deliverance of the city, when he commissioned the church in 1716. Happily St Charles was not only popularly invoked in times of plague (in fact, since his role in the great plagues in Milan of 1570 and 1576), but he was also the namesake of the emperor. In the church, Fischer von Erlach strove to create a truly imperial style of Baroque architecture and it remains a curiously isolated phenomenon with few forebears and no obvious successors. The foundation stone was laid in 1716 but by Fischer von Erlach's death in 1723 the structure was still incomplete, and under his son Joseph Emanuel considerable modifications were introduced. However an indication of Fischer von Erlach's intentions can be gained from the series of engravings in his book *Historic Architecture . . .* when it was published in its enlarged form in 1721. In addition, the full impact of the church has now been lost, for today it is hemmed in by buildings on most sides and is approached across a maze of roads and tramlines. Bernardo Bellotto's view shows it standing in the fields outside the city when it was possible to walk right round it and savour the ever-changing relationships between the various elements. But above all it is the remarkable façade that endows the church with a rich variety, a dynamism and a unique grandeur.

The façade forms a gigantic independent screen in front of the church, attached to it for less than twenty per cent of its length; this in itself is a remarkable innovation only hinted at in Fischer

Bernardo Beliotto's painting of the Karlskirche showing its setting 1758–61. Fischer von Erlach designed the church to be seen from all angles, and much of its impact has been lost now that it is hemmed in by buildings on most sides.

The side elevation and section engraved in Fischer von Erlach's Entwurf einer historischen Architektur . . . *of 1721. These engravings reveal the substantial modifications made by Joseph Emanuel Fischer von Erlach to his father's designs, particularly in the alteration of the position of the subsidiary dome over the choir and the organisation of the decoration.*

Prospect
Vue de l'Eglise de S.¹ Charles Borromée au dehors
Der Kirchen S.¹ Caroli Borromæi von außen gegen Mittag.
Vers le Midi

Durchschnitt
Profil et Elevation de la Coupe de l'Eglise de S.¹ Charles
Der S.¹ Caroli Kirchen von einwendig wie solche anßusehen.
Borromée dans le dedans depuis l'Entrée nusqu au Chœur

105

Above, a detail of the right-hand column showing scenes from the life of St Charles Borromeo, to whom the church is dedicated. These columns are derived from Trajan's column in Rome, but their use in the Karlskirche is unique.

Left, the dome and the façade seen from the Karlsplatz. The oval plan of the dome is not immediately apparent, but it does give the dome the additional strength needed to dominate the side elevations.

von Erlach's Dreifaltigkeitskirche in Salzburg (1694). However it enabled him to manipulate the elements in a far freer and more sculptural fashion than had ever been possible for the Roman High Baroque architects. The central section consists of a relatively low classical portico with a curious attic storey, set slightly back from the pediment, carrying four large allegorical statues, while the apex of the pediment carries a group of the Apotheosis of St Charles Borromeo. Behind this a modified palace façade curves strongly backwards to join up with the low square towers at each end of the façade, while into the curves snuggle the two huge column motifs, which frame the oval dome behind. The references to Rome are unmistakable and yet the result is totally un-Italian; it is as much a critique of Italian High Baroque architecture as a development from it.

St Peter's lies at the root of the design, but Fischer von Erlach has also drawn on the façade of S. Agnese in Piazza Navona, in itself a High Baroque reworking of Bernini's schemes for the façade of St Peter's, and the change in relative values of the various elements is revealing. In S. Agnese the concave façade draws all lines of force towards the central doorway and firmly links the towers with the central section and the dome. But in the Karlskirche the curved bays lead away from the central portico instead of towards it, and the main door is relatively insignificant. The portico juts forward, and the lines of force tend to move outwards to the low corner towers, and great emphasis is laid on the length of the façade. Juvarra's Superga (1717–31), which is almost an exact contemporary, provides a fascinating contrast with a closely comparable scheme; there the emphasis is on verticality with a static balance based on classical poise and restraint. Fischer von Erlach's façade, however, depends on a vigorous dynamic balance and the pairs of columns play a crucial role. If the various elements are examined separately it may be felt that the façade is too long and too low, and that the dome is too heavy for the light portico. But the strong verticality of the columns counteracts the horizontality of the façade and takes over the role of the towers in framing the dome. Further, the relationship between the component parts is additionally complicated by the lack of any formal link between the columns and the rest of the façade; the building is unthinkable without them and yet they perform no recognisable function outside the realms of symbolism and aesthetics.

These columns with their spiral relief decorations are derived

Above, the groundplan of the Karlskirche emphasising the most unusual relationship between the long façade and the body of the church behind. In some respects the layout is influenced by S. Maria della Salute in Venice, particularly in the placing of the High Altar.

107

from Trajan's column in Rome; they are carved with scenes from the life of St Charles Borromeo, but their symbolic role is derived from the pair of columns that traditionally flanked the entrance to the Temple of Solomon. Unlike Trajan's column, each is topped by a tall lantern bearing a gilt imperial crown and the square bases from which these lanterns rise are decorated with gilt imperial eagles. (An additional source may have been provided by Paris Bordone's painting of a gladiatorial combat, which was in the collection of Charles VI; this includes a Pantheon-like structure with a portico flanked by a pair of Trajan columns. It has also been suggested that they were inspired by eastern minarets or by Sangallo's church of S. Maria di Loreto; none of these suggestions diminishes the originality of Fischer von Erlach's achievement.

Carl Gustav Heraeus was responsible for the programme of decoration. We have already referred to the group of the Apotheosis of St Charles Borromeo over the pediment. The lower attic storey behind carries four allegorical figures, while Faith and Hope crown the side towers and two large angels at ground level either side of the entrance flight of steps symbolise the Old and New Testaments. Further angels are seated on each side of the oval windows piercing the dome, and with the pairs of flaming urns they add richness to the base of the dome. The drum itself has a complex system of articulation because the windows on the longitudinal axis are, rather surprisingly, flanked by paired pilasters while those on the transverse axis are flanked by single pilasters. Those on the diagonal axes have no flanking pilasters, but each unit is separated by a pair of attached columns, set forward, which are continued by the ribs of the dome. This means a greater emphasis is laid on the sections of the drum that lie on the longitudinal axis than those that lie on the transverse axis, with a resultant tendency to reduce the effect of the oval form.

The oval form of the dome is relatively unimportant for the exterior of the church and the body of the church is completely concealed by the façade; but inside the dome dominates the entire structure. Again the Dreifaltigkeitskirche at Salzburg provided Fischer von Erlach's prototype and the plan consists of a large longitudinal oval, which is preceded by an entrance bay and leads in turn through a choir space. The transverse axis of the main oval space opens up into a pair of large rectangular side chapels with galleries above, which are oval in plan. How much Joseph Emanuel altered his father's plans is arguable, but he had clearly taken over

Above, the interior of the dome showing the frescoes by Johann Michael Rottmayr, which depict St Charles Borromeo interceding with the Virgin Mary on behalf of the people of Vienna. The illusionistic architectural surround, painted by Gaetano Fanti, continues the real architecture into the painted world above.

Left, the façade and dome. Frontally, the oval dome is more vertical in its effect, and a complex dynamic balance is created between it, the flanking towers, the columns and the portico. In the Karlskirche Fischer von Erlach strove to create a truly imperial style.

109

Left, the interior of the main congregation space looking towards the High Altar. The space is articulated with giant Corinthian pilasters in purplish marble, standing on high pedestals as favoured by Palladio, and these carry the entablature which forms the ring below the drum of the dome.

the supervision of Fischer von Erlach's buildings well before 1723 and there are substantial differences between the engraved designs and the building as completed. However, these differences are mainly in the decoration and where they are structural they are in the higher zones, suggesting that Joseph Emanuel had greater freedom as the building progressed.

Fischer von Erlach articulated the main oval space with a giant order of Corinthian pilasters on high pedestals in the Palladian manner, and had intended the sides of the entrance arch to be articulated with pairs of free-standing Ionic columns, backed with pilasters and carrying a short length of heavy entablature supporting pairs of figures. The same motifs were to be repeated in the entrances to the main side chapels and again at each end of the choir space. These were modified during building and in the choir replaced by attached half columns, while all the statues were abandoned in favour of flaming urns (as also happened on the outside of the dome where the ribs meet the coupled columns). However, the most drastic alterations from the engraved designs are again to be found in the choir area, which Fischer von Erlach had intended to be vaulted by a small cupola leaving the high altar in relative shadow. Further, there was to have been a low retro-choir behind the high altar, separated from the body of the church by a Palladian screen of columns, and the high altar would have been silhouetted against the light beyond in a manner strongly reminiscent of S. Maria della Salute. In execution, however, the entire system was altered. The cupola was moved back so that it now lights the altar space leaving the choir in relative darkness, while the retro-choir has been abandoned and the lower part of the high altar is now solid.

Light now pours down from the cupola with such intensity that the function of the window behind the sunburst is almost lost, and the Berninesque vigour of Fischer von Erlach's design totally emasculated.

Further substantial alterations were made to the drum and the dome, finished 1724, when Joseph Emanuel raised the height of the dome, replaced the rectangular windows of the drum with a round-headed type and added the pilasters to the exterior. Inside, relatively small changes drastically altered the character and it can only be assumed that Joseph Emanuel was also responsible for these. Fischer von Erlach had intended that the entablature over the large arches on the main axes, with their flanking pilasters, should break forward to form triumphal arch motifs repeated round the interior, and that the pilasters articulating the drum should rise naturally from these motifs and continue upwards through the ribs of the vault to the ring of the cupola. This carefully thought-out system, in part inspired by S. Andrea al Quirinale, was abandoned in the finished church and instead the sections of

The side chapels flanking the congregation space. The side walls of the main chapels are articulated with pairs of Ionic columns, and in a modified form the same are repeated by the principal doorway and at the entrance to the choir. However, these were intended by Fischer von Erlach to support the pairs of figures which were later abandoned in favour of the flaming urns seen today.

111

the entablature on the diagonal axes break forward. Cohesion between the giant order and the pilasters between the windows of the drum is lost and Fischer von Erlach's subtle but harmonious system rejected. Additional problems are raised by the decoration of the dome, since Fischer von Erlach originally intended this to be coffered not painted, and the frescoes were not executed until 1727–30. In fact, Fischer von Erlach probably intended the entire interior of the church to be white, as in the Kollegienkirche, which would have resulted in a powerful but cold grandeur, but Joseph Emanuel's use of red and pink marbles reflects the change in taste that took place at the end of the first quarter of the 18th century, demanding a much richer and less ascetic effect.

Johann Michael Rottmayr's fresco reflects the same change in taste and a progressive lightening of his palette is seen during the last decade of his life (he died in 1730). Although the individual figures remain strongly sculptural, the composition is much looser and more decorative than his earlier frescoes in the Matthiaskirche at Wroclaw (1704–06) or Melk (1719). The illusionistic architectural surround, or *quadratura*, was painted by the Bolognese specialist Gaetano Fanti, but compared to earlier ceiling paintings, in particular that in Fischer von Erlach's Ahrensaal at Schloss Vranov (1690–94), it performs a much more decorative function and the illusion is less obtrusive. Rottmayr and Fanti co-operated in the decoration of the subsidiary vaults of the Karlskirche, and these are thematically linked to the main vault where St Charles Borromeo with the Virgin Mary intercedes on behalf of those afflicted by the plague. They float on a cloud while nearby a group of putti display St Charles's cardinal's hat and his staff as archbishop of Milan. Above, Christ adds his support and God the Father blesses the symbolic globe supported by putti below; the vault of the cupola above is painted with the dove.

The main vault fresco depicts St Charles Borromeo in heaven, while the high altar represents an earlier stage during the apotheosis of the saint. Here the design was by Fischer von Erlach and the execution by Lorenzo Mattielli (1688–1748) from Vicenza, and the white and gold figure of the saint, supported on clouds, is carried upwards by angels and putti against a background of coloured marble. Above the altar a gigantic sunburst of gilt rays, centred on the sacred inscription, bursts through the wreath of white stucco clouds, angels and putti. A cluster of rays extends down to the figure of the saint, linking the composition together, while the pairs of

Above, the north side altar with the Assumption of the Virgin painted by the Venetian, Sebastiano Ricci in 1734. His lightness of handling and brilliant colours are in direct and welcome contrast to the massive grandeur of the architecture.

112

The focal point of the church is provided by the group over the High Altar depicting St Charles Borromeo carried up to heaven in glory by angels and putti. Designed by Fischer von Erlach, the white and gold stucco figures were executed by Lorenzo Mattielli.

massive columns on each side are crowned by stucco figures of the four Doctors of the Church, who bear witness to the inscription. The reference to Bernini's Cathedra Petri in St Peter's is clear, while the lower section is derived from reliefs such as Caffa's *Ecstasy of St Catherine* in S. Caterina in Montemagnapoli in Rome, but the synthesis afforded an extremely illusionistic ensemble, which was to find few imitators in Austria. In the Karlskirche Fischer von Erlach succeeded in his aim to create the model for a truly imperial Baroque style, despite the modifications of his son Joseph Emanuel. Unfortunately it was these alterations, so remote from the intellectual austerity of his father, that caught the imagination of Austrian architects and not the monumentality and grandeur sought by Fischer von Erlach.

113

Sv. Mikuláš, Malá Strana, Prague

Sv. Mikuláš dominates the quarter of Prague, known as Malá Strana or Kleinseite, which nestles below the Hradčany in the narrow strip between it and the river Vltava. Otakar II in 1257 cleared the area as a market place and founded a small parish church in the centre; it was this site that was given to the Jesuits after the Thirty Years War. Work began on the stolid monastery buildings in 1665, and in 1673 the foundations were laid for a new church. However, work soon stopped and by 1703 it had been restarted on a new plan. The nave was vaulted in 1711 and, after a temporary wall had been built closing the east end, work stopped again. These bald facts summarise the little that is known for certain about the first stage of the building of one of the most exciting Baroque churches in Europe, and since the architect is not recorded one must turn to the building itself for further data.

The three-bay nave forms an almost autonomous unit with large bevelled arches separating it from the entrance bays and the later choir and sanctuary, and basically the design follows the Vorarlberg pattern of wall-pillar churches. However it is in the treatment of the wall-pillars themselves that Sv. Mikuláš differs so drastically from the usual churches of this type. Instead of the wall-pillars being faced with pilasters or columns aligned parallel to the axis of the nave, the pillars are bevelled at 45 degrees and the pilasters are aligned at this angle on the faces so formed. Further, the pilasters are doubled and superimposed so that they form vigorous re-entrant angles on the edges of the pillars and this system is reversed in the plinths and strong entablature where the front edge is rounded. All these devices make the pillars very sculptural, and an undulating motion is set up along the length of the nave, enhanced by the

The dome and tower of Sv. Mikuláš completely dominate Malá Strana in Prague, dwarfing the surrounding houses. Kilian Ignác Dientzenhofer added these to his father's church, 1737–53, during the second period of building.

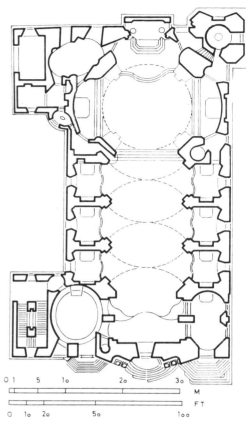

serpentine forms of the galleries. These are continued across the entrance bays by the organ gallery to form a single sinuous movement extending round the interior, broken only by the vertical accents of the pilasters.

Kracker's fresco on the vault was painted over half a century later, and for the architect's original intentions one must turn to the two drawings for the church, now preserved at Rheingau. These show that the architect intended the vault to be divided up by great swinging flat ribs rising from the tops of the pilasters and touching in the centre of the vault of each bay before continuing down to the pilasters on the opposite side of the nave to that where they started. In addition, these ribs form in plan a series of intersecting ovals, which march down the nave unifying the entire composition. An additional complication was added to the scheme by the fact that the arches between the piers penetrate well into the
116 vault and the triangular areas between these arches and the ribs are

Above, groundplan of Sv. Mikuláš. Christoph Dientzenhofer's church ended with a temporary wall at the last bay of the nave, and Kilian Ignác exploited all the space available beyond to create the great choir with its dome above.

Above left, the façade built by Christoph Dientzenhofer, 1703–11. His debt to Borromini's S. Carlo alle Quattro Fontane is clear but the façade here has been softened and given an almost mellifluous quality.

Right, the view into the choir space with the gigantic figures of the Fathers of the Church carved by Ignác František Platzer in 1769.

117

strongly concave, while the top of the vault is flat. Stylistically, the design of the pillars and these ideas for the vault support a firm attribution to Christoph Dientzenhofer, and the nave of Sv. Mikuláš can be compared closely to his church of Sv. Marketá at Břevnov, built in 1708–15, where the same principles are applied, although on a considerably smaller scale.

Christoph Dientzenhofer (1655–1722) can be first traced as an independent architect when working at the monastery of Teplá in 1689. It is thus with surprise that we learn from the monastic records that this brilliant architect was totally unable to read or write, and the problem of his sources becomes all the more acute. Despite attempts by some scholars to show that Christoph Dientzenhofer evolved his style independently of Guarini, the weight of the evidence still points to him as the key figure in the introduction of this type of architecture into Bohemia. Guarini's plans for the church of the Virgin of Alt-Ötting in Prague were apparently accepted in 1679, but these were never carried out and it is doubtful whether the Theatine Father ever visited Prague. His *Dissegni d'architettura*, published in 1686, was a far more potent source of ideas.

The rhythmic articulation of the nave of Sv. Mikuláš is closest to Guarini's church of the Divine Providence in Lisbon, of which a series of engravings is included in his book, though earlier examples of this type of planning can be cited in Bohemia. The nave of the Divine Providence in Lisbon was strongly undulating and, in contrast to Guarini's designs for Prague, cross ribs were abandoned and the whole vault was constructed on a system of diagonal ribs only. This also resulted in an undulating vault, linked continually with the pilasters below, but as is characteristic of Guarini, the two zones were firmly separated by a heavy entablature. A clear debt to this design is to be seen in the abbey church at Obořiště, which is almost certainly by Christoph Dientzenhofer. The plans were accepted in 1702, and there the two zones are firmly separated by a heavy entablature, but in his church of Sv. Klára at Cheb, begun in 1708, the entablature is broken into small sections separated by windows as at Břevnov.

Guarini's ribs only curve in two dimensions, and Christoph Dientzenhofer's vital innovation in the nave vault of Sv. Mikuláš was to introduce ribs curved in three dimensions, such as had been previously hinted at only in Guarini's centrally planned churches. To a great extent this was inspired by the complex Late Gothic

118

Above, the interior of the choir space of Sv. Mikuláš. Kilian Ignác Dientzenhofer assembled the architectural elements together in such profusion that the wall surface seems to vanish under the mass of balconies, niches and doorways. The heavy plasticity of this lower zone gives way to a much lighter handling in the drum of the dome.

Right, the bays of the nave are linked together by the gallery which undulates round the interior, and the pilasters, set obliquely on the wall-pillars, give strength to this rhythmic articulation. The gigantic figures of Jesuit saints and virtues were carved by Ignác František Platzer, about 1755.

vaulting systems of churches such as Sv. Barbara at Kutná Hora, which had reached their most advanced forms in Bohemia during the early 16th century. The original decoration of the nave vault of Sv. Mikuláš was most probably very similar to that of Břevnov, in both design and crudity, and the Kracker fresco provides a much more subtle composition.

Christoph Dientzenhofer's façade is the other important element belonging to the 1703–11 period of construction, and while the interior of the nave looks to Guarini the façade is clearly indebted to Borromini as well. The tightly articulated and intensely dynamic façade of S. Carlo alle Quattro Fontane has here been softened and given an almost mellifluous quality. Christoph Dientzenhofer has avoided giving the façade a strong central accent by reversing the convex forms of the central bay before they become too insistent, and the large central window acts as an oasis in the middle of these restless forms. Like the nave, the façade is imbued with a slow undulating rhythm, which extends across its entire width, but, as is characteristic of most Late Baroque architecture, there is no climax. All the elements vie with one another in importance, and the effect is richly pictorial rather than sculptural.

Above, the organ gallery which closes off the west end of the nave and links the galleries to each side. The large fresco with its dramatic illusionistic rendering of the architecture was painted by František Xaver Palko and his assistant, Josef Hagen.

Right, Richard Prachner and his son Petr were responsible for the magnificent pulpit (1766) which was based on contemporary Bavarian designs. Their studio in Prague was second only in importance to that of I. F. Platzer.

Left, the dome of Sv. Mikuláš, frescoed by the Silesian-born painter, František Xaver Palko, was completed in 1753. His design is rather restrained and conservative, despite his light colours, and looks back for its model to Rottmayr's fresco in the Karlskirche. Vienna.

Christoph Dientzenhofer died in 1722 before his designs for the choir and tower could be carried out, and it was left to his son Kilian Ignác to complete the church in 1737–53. Instead of the short transverse rectangular choir vaulted by a low dome without a drum intended by Christoph, the new design was much grander and the high dome and tower were intended to become the focal point of Malá Strana. Kilian Ignác decided to make use of all the available space at the choir end of the site, and abandoned Christoph's plans for a large sacristy behind the high altar. Instead, he designed an oval sacristy adjoining the left-hand side of the high altar while the entire right-hand side was to be occupied by the almost solid masonry of the base of the gigantic tower. The area under the dome is treated as a centrally planned space with three semicircular apsidal lobes, and although the dome is carried on massive piers and orthodox pendentives, the handling of these piers is unusual.

Each pier is articulated by coupled columns, but instead of the columns having a structural function they are set forward and carry only elaborate crowning motifs and allegorical sculpture. The sides of the piers are articulated with superimposed pilasters of the same size, carrying a heavy entablature, which breaks

Above right, one of the greatest triumphs of Baroque monumental painting north of the Alps is the huge fresco on the nave vault painted by Johann Lukas Kracker, 1760–61. Dominating the fresco is the gigantic triumphal arch over the grave of St Nicholas of Myra, while, above, the saint is carried up to heaven.

Below right, a detail of the fresco, including a self-portrait of the painter reclining in front of a column.

forward over the coupled columns. This intrusion into the space under the dome is further emphasised by the four figures of the Fathers of the Latin Church, who stand on consoles projecting from the pedestals, and by the figures on each side of the high altar, which repeat the motif. The massive structure of the high altar niche containing the figure of St Nicholas adds to the heavy plasticity of the lowermost zone of the structure; so many balconies, niches, doorways and other elements are added in rich profusion that the wall surface entirely disappears.

Kilian Ignác deliberately exploited this overwhelming, if not oppressive, effect to create a strong contrast with the higher zones. The eye, like the soul, turns upwards to seek repose in the heavenly regions of the dome. Above the entablature the space seems to open out rather than close in, and the windows of the drum are separated by pairs of slender columns with figures on consoles in which the same elements as below are used again to create an entirely different effect. Heavy plasticity has given way to a much more lyrical key, particularly in the curiously twisted plinths of the urns.

The tower and dome can be properly seen only from a distance and from every angle they loom over the sea of roofs of Malá Strana, the plump mass of the drum and dome contrasting with the virile, sharply cut forms of the tower, almost like a pair of dancers. It is only when the church is viewed from close quarters that their enormous height becomes apparent and the observer notices with surprise that the tower stands on a high basement and is articulated with four full orders without any sense of monotony, while it is linked to the façade by the rippling cornice and entablature extending the length of the church.

The third and last great period of activity in the church dates from 1760–61 when Johann Lukas Kracker frescoed the vaults. What Kilian Ignác Dientzenhofer achieved architecturally on the exterior of the church, binding all the units together into a single vibrant organic whole, Kracker achieved in the interior, and the great nave fresco is one of the finest expressions of Baroque monumental painting north of the Alps. Christoph Dientzenhofer's ribs were plastered over to form a single smooth undulating surface, and in the lowermost zones the painted architecture follows and develops the forms below. Above rearing classical porticos, ruined towers and glimpses of landscape give way to the open sky and a cluster of angels carrying St Nicholas up to heaven and the fresco acts as a grand finale to the church below.

Vierzehnheiligen

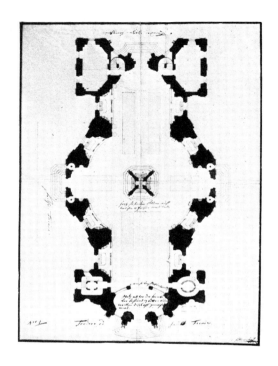

After Die Wies the pilgrimage church of Vierzehnheiligen is probably the best known 18th-century church in Central Europe, and like Birnau it was a Cistercian foundation. The church is located on the spot in the valley of the Main where a miraculous vision of the 14 Nothelfer (Helpers in Need or Auxiliary Saints) with the Christ Child appeared to shepherds in 1445 or 1446. It soon became a place of pilgrimage, and in 1448 a small chapel was built there by the Abbot of Langheim. Vierzehnheiligen continued to belong to the abbey of Langheim and the decision to replace the Gothic chapel with a splendid Baroque church was taken in 1735. However, the selection of an architect was the cause of an unedifying quarrel between Stephan Mösinger, the Abbot of Langheim, and Friedrich Carl von Schönborn, the Prince-Bishop of Bamberg.

In 1739 Mösinger gave the commission to Gottfried Heinrich Krohne (1703–56), a weak architect and the Surveyor General of the Protestant Duke Ernst August I of Saxe-Weimar. Krohne produced a centralised design in the tradition of the Frauenkirche at Dresden, while the exterior of the building, from a drawing in Nuremberg, was to have been a curiously hybrid structure with the low dome topped by a large globe. Other plans were also submitted by Maximilian von Welsch, whose design was derived from the Gesù, and Neumann's assistant in Bamberg, Jacob Michael Küchel. Küchel's proposals were far more in sympathy with the nature of the commission, and the scheme for placing the free-standing altar to the 14 Nothelfer in the centre of the church under an oval dome was conceived by him.

Friedrich Carl von Schönborn was in favour of Balthasar

Above, Jacob Michael Küchel's proposals for Vierzehnheiligen are embodied in this groundplan with variations now preserved in the Germanisches National-Museum in Nuremberg. Most important was Küchel's idea of planning the shrine dedicated to the Fourteen Nothelfer under a central dome.

Opposite, the pilgrimage church of Vierzehnheiligen, overlooking the valley of the Main. The elegant, almost Gothic proportions of the façade are characteristic of Balthasar Neumann, as is the superb handling of the architectural details.

125

Neumann and in 1743 the commission was transferred to him. The plan submitted by Neumann was based on a Latin cross with a drumless dome over the crossing, and this dome was to have been supported by groups of three free-standing columns instead of piers, developing the scheme he used at Etwashausen. The shrine of the 14 Nothelfer was to have been located under the crossing and in the same relationship to the high altar as the baldacchino in St Peter's. Mösinger accepted this new plan, but turned it over to Krohne to execute, with disastrous results. For Krohne began the foundations and the construction of the choir too far up the hill, and ruined the design by making it impossible for the shrine to be placed under the crossing. Friedrich Carl made vigorous complaints, and Neumann was left with the problem of redesigning the interior of the church to meet the new conditions.

The design of the church as built is a brilliant compromise, which snatched victory from the jaws of defeat, rather than a wilful exercise in complexity for its own sake. Neumann took over Küchel's idea of the shrine in the centre of the church and re-designed the system of vaulting so that this area became the centre of the composition and the crossing was reduced to little importance. The groundplan is of great complexity and differs significantly from that of the vaulting, but in basis it consists of a succession of three longitudinal ovals forming the nave and the choir, and two circles forming the transepts. Superimposed on this system are two transverse ovals, which form the crossing and the area between the entrance bay and the central area of the nave. But while the organisation of the order and entablature emphasise these transverse ovals, they are rejected in the vaulting system above. An additional element of complexity is the pair of longitudinal oval side chapels off the nave, which again break down the autonomy of the transverse ovals and extend into the low side aisles.

At first glance, on entering, the church seems to be symmetrical about the central area of the nave and the shrine, but the complexity of the planning is too great to be taken in from any single point and the regular patterning of the floor gives no assistance. Light floods into the church through three tiers of windows, but the walls and glass seem to melt away leaving only the coloured *scagliola* columns and the intricate vaulting, in a manner that echoes Gothic architecture. The high windows in the zone of the vaulting are probably best described as clerestory windows, while the galleries below look as much to Gothic triforia as to any other

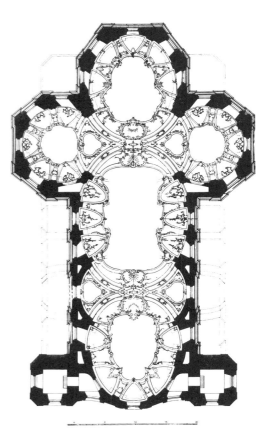

Above, the vaulting plan of Vierzehnheiligen, revealing its independence of the groundplan. The main vaults extend into the areas of the crossing and nave chapels so that these spaces have no real significance of their own.

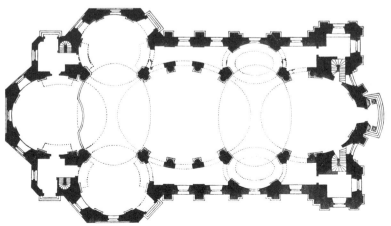

Above, a general view of the interior of Vierzehnheiligen with the shrine of the Fourteen Nothelfer in the foreground and the High Altar behind. Light pours through the many large windows and sparkles on the plasterwork giving the effect of a fairy-tale world of icing sugar.

Left, the groundplan consists of a series of intersecting ellipses and circles which are in complete contrast to the straight outlines of the exterior. Balthasar Neumann skilfully reduced the importance of the crossing and instead brought the design to a focus on the shrine under the central vault.

127

sources. As has been pointed out in the introduction, Balthasar Neumann's debt to Gothic architecture is considerable and this is even more plainly visible in the exterior of Vierzehnheiligen. The Gothic quality of the interior has also been emphasised by the decoration, and in particular by the Rococo stucco work lavished on the vaults while the walls are left almost entirely bare.

The central oval is formed by sets of four three-quarter columns on high pedestals attached to piers on each side of the nave with galleries inserted at about half the height between the entablature and the ground. The three bays on each side, so formed, are continued into the vaulting zone by the clerestory windows and, by the omission of the gallery in the choir and transepts, this system is carried round the interior of the church. However, the piers flanking the nave side chapels, as well as those of the crossing, are articulated with additional pilasters in coloured *scagliola* in order to maintain the centrality of the composition, and from them spring the broad panelled ribs which differentiate the various areas of the vaulting. These ribs are not structural and they twist across the vaults marking the boundaries between the longitudinal oval *platzlgewölbe*, the dissected circular *platzlgewölbe* of the transepts and the small triangular vaults, all that remain of the transverse oval vaults.

Everywhere the emphasis is on curving lines and complex intersecting curved surfaces; even the shafts of the *scagliola* pilasters are concave. The church of Vierzehnheiligen was to some extent built in rivalry to the church of Banz, constructed by Johann Dientzenhofer in 1710–18 on a hill on the opposite side of the Main, and the two provide a revealing contrast in the use of ribs. At Banz the powerful curved and jutting forms of the nave order are linked together by heavy flat ribs in a thoroughly Guarinesque scheme, but at Vierzehnheiligen in the 1740s these ribs are used much more delicately and lose their structural significance entirely. The ribs meet over the centre of the crossing, which without a vault of its own, ceases to be a spatial unit of any consequence; the area between the nave side chapels received the same treatment. As a result of these multiple interpenetrations, it becomes impossible to dissociate any one space from the remainder of the building, and the interior is possessed of a strong organic unity which, despite the Rococo decorations, is fully Baroque in its implications.

Jacob Michael Küchel was responsible for the execution of Neumann's designs and fully understood his former master's ideas, including the use of reinforced concrete in the vaulting. After

Above, the oval crossing area is deprived of autonomy by the extension of the vaults of the adjacent areas, so that in effect it has no vault of its own. This apparent lack of continuity between the groundplan and the vaulting is one of the factors which makes this interior so exciting visually.

Left, the vaulting of the second bay of the nave follows that of the crossing, and the various different curved surfaces are defined by broad flat bands of decoration which curve in three dimensions.

129

Left, the brothers Johann Michael and Franz Xaver Feichtmayr with Johann Georg Übelherr were responsible for the superb sculpture and plasterwork by which Küchel's ideas were brought to final fruition after Neumann's death in 1753.

Neumann's death in 1753, he continued to supervise the construction of the building until his own death in 1769, and the church was almost completed by 1772. The designs for the shrine, high altar, and pulpit are all those of Küchel after Neumann's death, and both the quantity and the character of the decoration of the remainder of the church reflect his tastes rather than those of Neumann. The most important of these is the shrine, or Nothelferaltar, which acts as the focal point of the interior. This most ornate and elegant structure is designed almost as a piece of abstract sculpture. The upper part is a synthesis of the forms of a Baroque state coach with those of Bernini's baldacchino; the splendid sunburst that crowns

Left, the High Altar, also designed by Johann Michael Küchel after 1753. Next to the central shrine this is the second focus of the design; the general layout with open side wings flanked by figures is inspired by the altar designs of Balthasar Neumann.

it includes four figures of the Christ Child, while four of the saints are seated on the corners. The lower part of this creation defies description, consisting of a system of Rococo scrolls and other elements in multi-coloured *scagliola*, with white and gold figures in niches seated on the scrolls. On three sides the structure is surrounded by a low circular balustrade with four further figures on plinths, aligned with the scroll forms, and on the fourth side this balustrade curves inwards to allow the worshipper to approach closely the shrine proper and the site of the vision. The remaining three concave faces of the shrine are occupied by altars to cater for the demands of the large numbers of pilgrims expected. The brothers Johann Michael and Franz Xaver Feichtmayr with Johann Georg Übelherr were responsible for the superb sculpture and plasterwork, which make Küchel's shrine one of the great monuments of the German Rococo.

From the central shrine vistas open up in all directions; the composition finds a second focus in the structure of the high altar,

132

Küchel's pulpit, designed to illustrate the theme of divine inspiration. The sounding board is replaced by a splendid sunburst with seven clusters of rays representing the seven gifts of the Holy Ghost. On the body of the pulpit below are carved the four evangelists who made these gifts known to the four continents, represented in turn by heads of putti.

also designed by Küchel. The open side wings flanked by figures and the general layout are inspired by Balthasar Neumann, and may be compared to Neumann's altars at Bruchsal, Trier, and elsewhere. J. M. and F. X. Feichtmayr were again responsible for the sculpture, and the figures are rather more restrained than the slightly earlier sculpture at Ottobeuren and Rott-am-Inn. The whole of the plaster decoration of the interior of the church is of the finest quality, but it has a lightness and vivacity, which is almost at odds with the severity of the architecture and in fact greatly reduces the impact of Neumann's ingenious handling of space. Particularly beautiful are the richly modelled capitals to the attached columns and pilasters, gilt in contrast to the pink *scagliola* of the shafts, and the splendid cartouches which break into the frescoes both over and under the frames. Much of the detail of this plasterwork is naturalistic with fruit and leaves, which appear to grow out of the *rocaille* forms. The frescoes and altarpieces are undoubtedly the weakest parts of the decoration, and for the most part the main frescoes were painted by Giuseppe Appiani in 1764–70. The altarpieces are even weaker, being mostly painted by A. Palme in the late 19th century, and are a sad anticlimax.

In 1803 the church was secularised and the Cistercians of Langheim dispersed, while the treasures and fittings of the church were plundered. Unfortunately in 1835 lightning struck the south tower of the façade, destroying the upper part of the tower, all the roofs and the western parts of the decoration of the interior including Georg Kramer's organ of 1770. Repairs were begun in 1838 and in the following year King Ludwig of Bavaria took over the care of the church and built the priests' house. The interior

A detail of the canopy, crowned with a sunburst and four figures of the Christ Child, over the shrine of the Fourteen Nothelfer. Scagliola can be modelled and polished into almost any configuration, and with the wide variety of bright colours possible, it proved the ideal material for the Rococo decorators.

was restored between 1845 and 1872 when the late altarpieces were added, and the interior was restored again in 1958. Finally the façade and towers were extensively restored in 1893–1910, giving the exterior of the church its present appearance.

The contrast between the interior and the exterior of Vierzehnheiligen could hardly be greater, though the exterior is by no means without interest and seen in the late afternoon light the golden yellow sandstone of which it is built seems to glow. Perhaps the most striking element is the extraordinarily strong verticality of the façade with its twin towers capped by elegant helms. The façade is articulated by two giant orders, the lower Doric with broad rusticated pilasters on high pedestals, and the upper Corinthian with smooth pilasters, again on high pedestals. The central bay of the façade is convex, framed by full columns and pillars instead of pilasters, and it is joined to the bays that form the bases of the towers by relatively narrow concave bays. A strong entablature separates the two storeys and adds a welcome horizontal element, while the upper order in the central bay is crowned by a broken pediment linked to the towers by a balustrade. The curiously Borrominesque pediment is carved in relief with the scene of the vision, and the figure of Christ the Redeemer stands on the apex.

To this already extremely high façade Neumann added the towers articulated with attached full Corinthian columns of the same size as the orders below, and high pointed helms. These give the façade the proportions and outline almost of a Gothic cathedral and it can hardly be doubted that Neumann had such buildings in mind. The façade almost dwarfs the remainder of the church, which, with its pronounced transepts and apse and its system of buttresses over the side aisles, presents a faintly archaic appearance.

The rusticated Doric pilasters of the lowermost storey of the façade are carried round the side aisles to the transepts and choir, where they take the form of vigorous quoins; this rustication forms a very effective contrast to the smooth ashlar of the remainder of the walls. In this lower order the two rows of windows are those seen above and below the galleries in the interior, while the upper order, which is only half the height of that on the façade and towers, corresponds to the clerestory windows penetrating the vaults inside. The cool precision of the forms and the immaculate quality of the masonry belong to the best tradition of Neumann's work and Vierzehnheiligen is undoubtedly his ecclesiastical masterpiece.

Weltenburg

Lying on the inside of a sharp bend of the Danube near Kelheim in Bavaria the monastery of Weltenburg is almost hidden by the hills that rise steeply from the river, and the austere buildings are a natural foil for the picturesque setting. A mission house is said to have stood on the site during the 7th century and this was developed into a monastery in 760 by St Boniface, the remarkable missionary from Devon who later became Archbishop of Mainz. Duke Tassilo II of Bavaria encouraged the saint and is thus revered as a founder, but the history of the foundation has been by no means uneventful and soon afterwards the monastery was destroyed by the Hungarian invasion. It recovered only to be devastated again centuries later by the Thirty Years War in 1632–33, while floods and ice floes also took their toll.

It was not until the appointment of Maurus Bächl as abbot (1713) that both the monastery buildings and the church were rebuilt. The former were constructed in 1714–25 to the designs of the Franciscan architect Philipp Plank (died 1720), and for the church Bächl turned to the brothers Cosmas Damian and Egid Quirin Asam. Apart from the tower of 1608, the old church was demolished in 1716 to make way for the present structure. The foundation stone was laid in the same year and for this venerable Benedictine foundation the Asams created one of the first, and finest, Baroque interiors in Bavaria.

Plank's buildings are grouped around a spacious courtyard and the church is built into the end of the wing on the east side, so that the façade seems to grow naturally from it and the severe exterior of the dome behind is almost disregarded. The façade is surprisingly restrained and static, and in total contrast to the robust curved

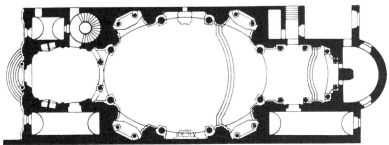

Above, the façade of the abbey church of
Weltenburg grows naturally out of the simple
earlier monastic buildings erected by Philip
Plank, 1714–25.

Left, Cosmas Damian Asam based his design on
a longitudinal oval congregation space linked to
a smaller choir and entered from a low entrance
hall. This relatively simple design provided the
basis for immensely rich decoration.

137

façades of the Karlskirche and of Weingarten, or the rippling movement of Sv. Mikuláš in Prague, all of which are almost exact contemporaries. Pilasters divide it up into three bays, but the large round-topped central window breaks through the entablature and extends well into the pediment. This creates a curious effect, since the façade takes on the character of a heavily modified triumphal arch and this same rhythm is employed again in the interior. As in the façade of Sv. Mikuláš there is a deliberate avoidance of a climax on the central line and the central bay is slightly recessed with this intention, while a rather more lively note is struck by the canted columns and broken pediment flanking the *oeil-de-boeuf* window over the entrance. In no way, however, does this quietly elegant façade give any hint of the sumptuous interior that awaits the visitor.

Basically the groundplan consists of a series of longitudinal ovals, with the first divided into two levels to provide a low entrance hall and space for the organ above. The heavy entablature sweeping round the interior of the congregation space breaks forward over the columns and pilasters that carry it and is continued round the organ space and choir, reaching its climax in the structure of the high altar. This system is derived from S. Giacomo degli Incurabili in Rome, but Cosmas Damian Asam avoided the conflict between the centrally planned space and the longitudinal axis that occurs there by the brilliantly simple expedient of replacing the usual semicircular arches by shallow segmental arches. Further, similar arches are repeated on the lateral axis of the congregational space and all four are partly masked by large pink stucco groups of the Evangelists and putti. These have the effect of further reducing the strength of these arches and, since the segmental forms are very shallow, the emphasis is laid on the immensely rich surface decoration of the coving of the cut-off dome.

The relatively restrained side altars on the diagonal axes are flanked by pilasters, instead of the full columns on the main axes, and they carry panelled ribs that divide up the coving. The decoration in this zone is clearly differentiated and the reliefs on the main axes are brilliantly gilt while those of the four archangels on the diagonal axes are depicted on elaborately diapered green and gold backgrounds. The only windows visible are the shallow segmental windows on the lateral axis and the rest of the lighting in the church is from concealed sources. Directed theatrical lighting, together with colour, are the key elements in the composition. These were

Egid Quirin Asam executed the High Altar between 1721 and 1724 to the designs of Cosmas Damian, and the group of St George and the Dragon is the focal point of the design. The equestrian group, brilliantly gilt and silvered, is silhouetted dramatically against the brightly lit fresco behind.

B.C.—6

Opposite, the entrance hall over which is the organ gallery with a pierced screen. As with the choir this space is separated from the main congregation space by a low segmental arch which hardly penetrates into the coving.

Left, not only St George but also the entire structure of the High Altar is silhouetted against the brightly lit fresco. He is flanked by figures of St Martin and St Maurus, while above an angel holds the electoral crown of Bavaria, wreathed in laurel, over the Bavarian coat of arms.

lessons learnt from Bernini in Rome, and it was the Asam brothers above all who took over the illusionistic ideas of Bernini and developed them to their fullest extent. The continual reminiscences in their work of Berninesque figures and motifs are perhaps only to be expected from artists who were his spiritual successors.

On entering the congregational space attention is drawn immediately by the strong lighting to the high altar and to the dome; in both the pale colours of the frescoes from a foil to the heavy gilding. In the congregation space the richness and exuberance of the stucco decoration on the coving gives way to a much more lyrical atmosphere above, where the shallow curved vault is frescoed with the Coronation of the Virgin in the presence of a host of saints. The action takes place under an illusionistically painted cupola, and this taste for strong architectural illusionism is characteristic of the early ceilings painted by C. D. Asam. A subsidiary centre of interest is provided by the figure of St George, depicted joining the host of saints, and this is thematically linked with the group of St George and the Dragon on the high altar, just as the musical figures such as St Cecilia and King David on the opposite side of the vault act as a link with the organ below. In addition St Peter, kneeling before the Virgin, is joined by St Benedict, the founder of the order.

For the design of the crown, through which the dome fresco is seen, the Asams turned to Borromini instead of Bernini, although it is a much lighter and more delicate affair, supported by putti and stucco clouds, than the heavy, attached crown motif of S. Carlo alle Quattro Fontane. The brilliant gilt stars of the crown sparkle in the sunlight, which streams in from concealed windows, and the whole structure is a witty allusion to the crown of stars of the Virgin in her role as Queen of Heaven. A more homely note is struck by the painted stucco figure of Cosmas Damian peering down into the church, which acts as one of the supports.

Brilliant though the dome decoration is, the high altar is undoubtedly the *tour-de-force* of the church. The triumphant equestrian group of St George, silhouetted against the fresco behind, strides through the archway into the church, while the dragon is transfixed by his lance and the princess recoils in horror. Egid Quirin executed the high altar between 1721 and 1724 from the designs of Cosmas Damian and the extreme theatricality of the ensemble marks a high point in his career. Bernini had included a curved fresco lit by concealed windows as the high altar in his

Egid Quirin Asam painted the shallow dome with the scene of St George, a victor's laurel wreath held above his head, welcomed into heaven by the Virgin. The strongly illusionistic treatment of the architecture is characteristic of the early date.

Left, one of the supports of the crown is provided by this self-portrait of Cosmas Damian Asam, modelled in stucco and painted in lifelike colours, and seen looking down into the church he created.

church at Ariccia, but the illusion is taken much farther by Egid Quirin and the entire structure of the altar is included in a single coherent scheme.

As in the dome fresco, there is a duality of subject matter. The altar fresco depicts the Glorification of the Virgin of the Immaculate Conception combined with the homage of the Bavarian Order of Knights of St George; the second subject is linked to the sculptured figures in the archway while the first is associated with the upper part of the fresco and the figures on top of the altar. Both themes are again brought together in the dome.

The group of St George and the Dragon is almost unparalleled in German Baroque art and it points to the Asams' great source of inspiration other than Bernini—Late Gothic sculpture. The realism and intense humanity of figures belong entirely to this fundamentally Northern tradition—a tradition mainly of wood-carving, which continued in the country areas throughout the 16th

Right, the vault fresco is seen through a gigantic gilt crown, which is supported from the coving; it glitters in the sunlight pouring in from the concealed windows. This crown is an allusion to the crown of the Virgin as Queen of Heaven.

and 17th centuries to blossom again in Southern Germany and Austria in the 18th century. It is the synthesis of the homely intimate qualities of Late Gothic sculpture with the theatrical grandeur of Bernini that gives the art of the Asams its peculiar strength. While Bernini's churches reflect the absolute power and magnificence of the papal court, the churches of the Asams, no less rich and gorgeous, are the product of the fervour and intense optimism of the people.

St George and the Dragon immediately invites comparison with the huge group by Bernt Notke in the church of St Nicholas in Stockholm (1489) and this type of Late Gothic group is clearly Egid Quirin's source of inspiration. Even so, the influence of Rome still asserts itself, since the figure of the saint and his horse are a close reworking of the statue of Marcus Aurelius on the Capitol! A strong contrast is created between St George and his horse, which are both entirely silvered and gilt and the princess and the dragon, which are painted in lively colours, while the multiple reflections of light off the equestrian group make it glitter like a gem in its setting and prevent it from being swamped by the brilliantly lit fresco behind. The archway is flanked on each side by spiral columns and strongly Berninesque gilt figures of St Martin and St Maurus. (St Maurus was happily a Benedictine saint who accompanied St Benedict to Montecassino.) These are linked to the central action by St Maurus (with the features of Abbot Bächl) who gazes up at St George while his bible and crozier are supported by a putto at his feet. St Martin, on the other hand, gestures towards the congregation that the faithful should take note of the sacred mystery enacted before it, while his goose arches its neck and hisses at the dragon.

Above the arch of the high altar an angel holds the electoral crown of Bavaria, wreathed in laurel, over the Bavarian coat of arms; this group acts as a rich centrepiece for the heavily gilt Corinthian capitals and swags to each side. The pediment is cleft in two and framed within it the stucco figure of the Virgin of the Assumption is carried up to heaven. Painted on the curved vault above and behind her, the figure of Christ waits to receive her into Heaven, while the stucco angels reclining on the broken pediment hand her a branch of roses and a sceptre. The composition is clearly inspired by Bernini's Apotheosis of St Andrew in S. Andrea al Quirinale, but here Egid Quirin has taken Bernini's ideas a stage further by locating a small round window behind.

On the diagonal axis the coving of the dome is decorated with high-relief figures of the four archangels. Here the brightly gilt figure of St Michael is seen against a richly patterned green and gold background, typical of the heavy Baroque style favoured by the Asam brothers.

From the congregational space this window is entirely masked by the top of the arch of the high altar so that light streams out into the choir past the figure of the Virgin, particularly in the morning.

The problem of the pulpit was solved most ingeniously by the Asam brothers when they integrated it into the north wall of the congregational space. A confessional occupies the lowermost zone of the wall, with rough decorative rockwork executed in stucco on each side while on top of the pulpit stands the figure of St Benedict preaching. The structure is then included within the large fresco illustrating the preaching activity of the Benedictine Order, and the frame grows out of the rockwork below. Both this fresco and that facing it, depicting the arrival of the first Benedictines in America in 1493, were extensively repainted in the 19th century

with a considerable loss of quality. Completion of the decorations was delayed until 1734–36, and the entrance hall was not finished until 1751, when Anton Neu freely interpreted the sketches of the Asam brothers for the confessionals and Cosmas Damian's son Franz Erasmus painted the ceiling (1745). The character of the plasterwork here (1734–36) is entirely different from that of the interior of the church proper and belongs to the fully developed Rococo style. The supreme lightness and vivacity, with gilding used sparingly to highlight points of special importance in the scheme, are very different in character to the heavy Baroque magnificence of the church decorations. In the contrast between the two lies the key to the change in spirit from the Baroque to Rococo and at the same time it marks the waning of the influence of Italy and its replacement by an essentially Northern style.

St Maurus gazes up at the figure of St George in the central archway of the High Altar. He was given the features of Abbot Maurus Bächl, who was responsible for the rebuilding of the church and monastery.

The rockwork round the confessionals on each side of the congregational space can again be traced to the Asams' studies of Bernini's designs in Rome. Above the confessional rises the pulpit, which is included, most ingeniously, within the fresco illustrating the preaching activity of the Benedictine Order.

149

Zwiefalten

The Karlskirche, Sv. Mikuláš, Vierzehnheiligen and Weltenburg, discussed in the four preceding chapters, characterise four of the most important trends in Baroque church architecture north of the Alps. The last chapters, however, are devoted to Rococo churches, all drawn from the much more limited area of Bavaria and Swabia. Pure Rococo churches, as opposed to Baroque churches with Rococo decorations, are a great deal less common than is often supposed and the vast majority are to be found in this area of Germany. The stucco decoration of Vierzehnheiligen is admittedly Rococo, as are most of the altars and other fittings, but these are applied to a structure whose fundamental characteristics are Baroque. In all his buildings Neumann intended the decoration to be strictly subordinated to the structure, but in the middle period of the activity of J. M. Fischer these principles were rejected, particularly at Zwiefalten and Ottobeuren.

In Rococo churches, any sense of dynamic structure is abandoned in favour of an overall sense of decorative unity. Rather surprisingly the seeds of such a dissolution of structure are to be traced to the decorative schemes of Bernini, though it is the change of spirit in the 18th century that is more important than any change in forms. Bernini and the Asams sought that total union of architecture with painting and sculpture, which is summed up in the German word *gesamtkunstwerk*, but always in their schemes Baroque dynamism binds the entire composition together and directs attention on to certain fixed points. The same synthesis of architecture and decoration is to be found in the best Rococo churches, but instead of Baroque dynamism a lighter, more lyrical tone prevails; the decoration spreads over the surfaces of the building until a total

The façade of Zwiefalten is chaste to the point of austerity, but J. M. Fischer's forceful use of simple elements gives it a certain grandeur. A more Rococo note is struck by the almost playful outline of the main pediment.

151

dissolution of structure takes place resulting in an insubstantial, almost fairy-tale effect. In Zwiefalten this process is well advanced, while in Steinhausen and Die Wies it reaches its climax.

The Benedictine Abbey of Zwiefalten was founded in 1089 at the instigation of Counts Kuno and Luithold and the original church was consecrated in 1109. The foundation steadily grew in wealth and importance, and in 1738 it was decided to rebuild the church. In 1740 the nave of the old church was demolished and the foundation stone of the new one laid, but the designs prepared by the abbey masons Josef and Martin Schneider ceased to satisfy the abbey authorities and in the following year Johann Michael Fischer was summoned instead. A new foundation stone was laid in 1744 and work progressed fast, since by 1747 the new church had been vaulted. The consecration did not take place until 1765, when the decoration was almost complete, but long before this Fischer's genius had been recognised in Swabia and his work at Zwiefalten had led, in 1748, to his gaining the commission for the rebuilding of the great abbey church of Ottobeuren.

On entering the church, the first impression is one of immense length and this effect is reinforced by the powerful and sombre frescoes on the relatively low vaults. At once it may be asked how much was Fischer influenced by the previous abbey church that occupied the site, and one is left with the strong suspicion that in the interests of economy he had to re-use the existing foundations. Certainly this hypothesis would do much to explain the almost tunnel-like effect of the church interior and the strange contrast between Zwiefalten and Ottobeuren. The design of the nave follows the wall-pillar type of church, with four bays divided by convex galleries and this leads into a central-crossing area vaulted with a saucer dome and flanked by deep transeptal spaces with

Despite the powerful and sombre frescoes, the effect of Zwiefalten is much lighter and more delicate than Weltenburg. Pale colours prevail below the vaulting and the brilliant rocaille *stucco decorations spread over the frescoes and structural elements alike.*

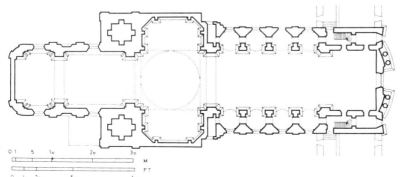

Left, the groundplan of Zwiefalten is surprisingly long and narrow for a church of this date; probably J. M. Fischer had to re-use the foundations of the medieval church in the interests of economy.

bevelled corners. The central space is entered from the nave through a slightly narrower archway, and in turn the entrance into the monks' choir is slightly narrower still, so that the choir and sanctuary follow the Vorarlberg pattern and are distinctly narrower than the nave. This layout, almost certainly the product of common sources rather than a free choice on the part of J. M. Fischer, has the perhaps unfortunate effect of still further emphasising the length of the church.

The nave piers are articulated with pairs of pink and pale blue-grey *scagliola* columns and these are carried round the remainder of the interior of the church to articulate the crossing piers, the transepts and the choir. Columns of the same coloured *scagliola*, on a slightly smaller scale, are used to articulate the high altar and transeptal altars. In overall effect these columns form a delicate contrast to the white plaster walls, and provide both a welcome upward movement and a foil for the extremely rich *rocaille* decoration. In the nave, the piers are set very close together and the galleries, as at Osterhoven (1726–40), are placed at a level just below the capitals, but the handling of these elements differs drastically. At Osterhoven J. M. Fischer made the piers concave with strongly bevelled edges so that a powerful sinuous rippling movement is created down the length of the nave reminiscent of Sv. Mikuláš, but at Zwiefalten these Baroque qualities are rejected in favour of a much more static system. Only the entrances to the side chapels under the galleries are bevelled and these are rigidly controlled by the massive *scagliola* columns. Further, the strength of the convex galleries is reduced by replacing the heavy balustrades with delicate wrought-iron work, and the capitals are designed as crisp rectangular forms echoing the form of the nave.

As at Osterhoven the nave bays are united together by a single large fresco, but, while C. D. Asam's fresco is firmly enclosed within a heavy undulating frame, Franz Josef Spiegler's vast mystical fresco of 1751 passes almost imperceptibly into Johann Michael Feichtmayr's stucco decorations. This rejection of Baroque dynamism and progressive dissolution of structure are characteristic of the Rococo style, and the detail handling of the frescoes themselves provides a fascinating contrast. At Osterhoven, as at Weltenburg, the illusionistic rendering of the architectural elements is taken to its logical conclusion. The painted architecture acts as an extension of the real world below and the illusion is made as convincing and forceful as possible. Nothing could be further from

In the vaults there is a progressive dissolution of structure as Franz Josef Spiegler's frescoes pass almost imperceptibly into Johann Michael Feichtmayr's stucco decorations. At the same time, Baroque dynamism is rejected in favour of lightness and vivacity.

155

Left, a typical detail of J. M. Feichtmayr's brilliant handling of stucco. Within the partly asymmetrical cartouche the putto pulls a long straggling rope of foliage, as if caught in the act of trying to put up a swag. Such wit and gaiety are characteristic of the Rococo.

this than Spiegler's fresco where the architectural elements are totally unreal and take on an almost viscous quality closely comparable to the writhing *rocaille* stucco decorations.

The gilt frame itself is so broken and capricious that it negates its purpose, and a wild riot of *rocaille* stucco decoration spreads over it and into the fresco itself. Above all swirl brown and ochre clouds as in the eye of a storm. The Trinity waits to receive into Heaven the Virgin, who is carried up on a cloud of angels and from whose heart a beam of light is directed at an image of the Virgin and Child, supported by more angels and putti. Another beam of light is directed from the heart of the Virgin in the image at the heart of St Benedict, which bursts into flame, and from him drops of fire cascade down on to the saints below. The meaning of this complex allegory is absolutely clear. The Virgin, by virtue of her special relationship with the Trinity, inflames the heart of St Benedict through his devotion to her image, and the saint in turn

Right, a gentle rhythmical movement is set up by the convex galleries down the sides of the nave, but in contrast to J. M. Fischer's nave at Osterhoven, the heavy coupled columns make the movement much less vigorous.

Left, Martin Hörmann from Villingen executed the decorative carving for the superb choir stalls in 1744, while the twenty large gilt reliefs depicting scenes from the life of the Virgin were carved by J. J. Christian.

imparts inspiration to the Benedictine saints and, by implication, the world below.

Without doubt the nave fresco is Franz Josef Spiegler's masterpiece, and the earlier frescoes by him at Zwiefalten have not quite the same freedom and fervour. The church was decorated from the choir working back to the nave, and the earlier choir and crossing frescoes of 1747 are much more firmly framed. In the crossing the Virgin is depicted in her role as Queen of Heaven, while over the monks' choir Spiegler painted *The Martyrdom of St Placidus and his Followers,* and over the high altar *The Virgin investing St Ildefonso with the Chasuble.* However the pendentives of the crossing dome are filled with superb *rocaille* stucco escutcheons by Feichtmayr, which frame frescoes depicting the four corners of the earth; this unusual iconography is maintained by the four groups below symbolising the elements.

J. M. Feichtmayr was also responsible for most of the statuary

Opposite, the gigantic mystical fresco painted on the nave vault by Franz Josef Spiegler in 1751. The complex allegory reveals the divine inspiration of St Benedict and how, through the Benedictine Order, this is imparted to the world in general.

159

in the church, for which he followed models provided by the sculptor Johann Joseph Christian. In the first quarter of the 18th century there was a tremendous demand for plasterers, who increasingly encroached on the domain of the sculptors. In 1725, however, an agreement was reached at Augsburg between the stonemasons' guild, to which the plasterers belonged, and the sculptors. From then on, independent sculpture was in theory to be the province of the sculptor, and if plasterers wished to execute such work a sculptor would have to be brought in. Lack of money as much as anything else led to the extensive use of stucco for the enormous quantity of sculpture required for the large 18th-century churches, and J. M. Feichtmayr collaborated with J. J. Christian at Ottobeuren as well as at Zwiefalten with conspicuous success. In addition, stucco is the ideal material for the flying draperies and extravagant poses increasingly demanded in the second quarter of the century and in turn, the use of such a flexible material encouraged further development in this direction.

Christian's and Feichtmayr's pulpit at Zwiefalten is one of the triumphs of German Rococo Art, and it is balanced by the *tableau* of Ezekiel on the opposite side of the entrance to the crossing space The theme of the pulpit is based on the complex relationship between sin and death, to which is wedded the vision of Ezekiel of the valley full of bones. At the base of the pulpit an angel with a flaming sword guards the forbidden tree, round whose trunk is coiled a serpent; above this, in a macabre *tableau*, Faith, Hope and Charity tend the dry bones, and those reclothed in flesh, seen by Ezekiel. On the canopy of the pulpit, Moses and John the Baptist flank the dead Christ, while at the foot of the cross the dove of the Holy Spirit is enshrined in a sunburst. The lower part of the pulpit thus symbolises man's death as a result of sin and eating the fruit of the forbidden tree, while the top part represents man's redemption by the death of Christ on the tree of the Cross. Death and resurrection are also the subject of the vision of Ezekiel, who is seen ecstatic on the other side of the church, and thus the two structures are thematically linked together.

Stylistically the thin, windswept draperies of Ezekiel and the angel with a flaming sword are in complete harmony with the wild *rocaille* decoration, and a further exotic note is provided by the extraordinary *rocaille* elements at the feet of Ezekiel and on the pulpit. These areas are covered with stucco that looks more like

dribbled multi-coloured sealing wax than the more normal motifs.

Two putti by J. J. Christian from the High Altar, 1748–49. J. M. Feichtmayr collaborated with J. J. Christian for the production of the larger figures, but the execution of these small putti may be by Christian alone.

Left, Ezekiel, modelled by J. M. Feichtmayr after a bozzette by J. J. Christian, is one of the most outstanding pieces of sculpture in the German churches of the 18th century. The extravagant windswept drapery emphasises the supernatural character of Ezekiel's vision.

The remainder of the decoration of the interior of the church is of exceptionally high quality, notably the superb choir stalls carved by Martin Hörmann from Villingen in 1744–52, including 20 reliefs of the Life of Mary by J. J. Christian, and the fine wrought-iron choir screen by Josef Büssel of 1751–57, while the excellent frescoes by the Viennese painter Franz Sigrist in the entrance hall (1760) strike a strangely alien note.

Compared to the interior of the church the façade of Zwiefalten is chaste to the point of austerity, but the forceful use of simple elements gives it a certain grandeur. The central doorway and the window are flanked by a single giant order of massive columns carrying a broken pediment, and their pedestals are treated as simple block forms. These elements are more strongly convex than the remainder of the façade and point the way to Ottobeuren. However, the austerity is greatly reduced by the almost playful outline of the main pediment and the brilliant figures of the Virgin and Child and St Benedict (1754) by J. J. Christian as well as by the delicate honey-coloured sandstone.

Right, the interior of Zwiefalten presents a curiously long, tunnel-like effect despite the importance given to the crossing area. However, the white plaster acts as a foil to the sombre frescoes, and the pink and white scagliola columns used throughout act as unifying elements.

Birnau

The visitor passing from Zwiefalten to Birnau becomes aware of a subtle change in flavour. The impact of Zwiefalten lies in the exquisite refinement of both the overall effect and the details; the character of Birnau is much more robust, and, despite the superb quality of much of the decoration, the church has an endearing, almost homespun character. This is typical of Swabian Rococo art, and this local variation on the Rococo style developed with relatively little influence from the Bavarian Court style.

Unlike most of the other churches described earlier, the structure was entirely new with no limitations placed on its location; the position was therefore carefully selected to make the best of the splendid site overlooking Lake Constance. Since the 13th century there had been a small shrine near Überlingen, further along the north shore of the lake, and this had contained a 'miraculous' statue of the Virgin, which had been tended by the monks of Salem since 1384. In the early 15th century, the chapel had been rebuilt and a new figure of the Virgin carved (today enthroned over the high altar at Birnau). In the 18th century, the monks decided to transfer the Virgin to a new church to be built on their own land and chose the present site beside the lake on the road between Überlingen and Meersburg. The first plans were submitted in 1741 by Johann Georg Stahl, the architect of Cardinal Damian Hugo von Schönborn, but in 1745 these were rejected in favour of the scheme proposed by the Vorarlberg architect Peter Thumb. In the following year the foundation stone was laid, and the church was dedicated in 1750, though many of the fittings were not finished for another eight years.

The west front faces the lake and the entrance bay to the church

The pilgrimage church of Birnau, close to the shore of Lake Constance, built by Peter Thumb, 1745–50. There is hardly any façade proper as the elegant tower is flanked by the twin blocks of the clergy house.

Left, Joseph Anton Feuchtmayer's statue of the Virgin occupies the niche over the main door. Carved from the same pink sandstone as the architectural details, her long thick neck and rather pudgy features are characteristic of Feuchtmayer's work.

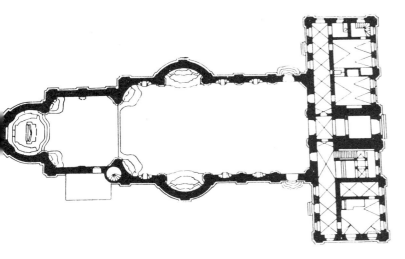

The groundplan of Birnau reveals the remarkable open interior achieved by Peter Thumb. Present-day visitors enter by the main door, but 18th-century pilgrims circulated through the pair of doors in the first bay of the nave.

is flanked by the twin blocks of the clergy house, so that the facade proper is more like that of a secular building than a church. Above it rises a single elegant tower, which is in contrast to the normal Vorarlberg tradition of twin towers, and it provides a subtle foil to the low pavilion forms of the clergy house. Originally it was intended that the church should be linked with the lake by a system of terraced gardens, but this was never carried out and one has reason to believe that the plans for Birnau were considerably reduced in scale.

Over the entrance portal there is a high window joined together into a single composition by an elegant balcony with wrought-iron rails, and this is surmounted by a niche containing a brilliant statue of the Virgin of the Immaculate Conception. Carved out of the same sandstone as the architectural details, she is shown in a strong twisting pose gazing over her right shoulder with her draperies billowing out on either side. Her long thick neck and rather pudgy features are characteristic of the style of Joseph Anton Feuchtmayer, while the handling of the drapery has curious echoes of 16th-century German prints.

This lower section of the tower is set slightly forward and articu-lated with giant pilasters, with the pavilions similarly set slightly forward from the linking sections and their corners articulated with giant pilasters of the same pattern. The remainder of the body of the church is articulated with further giant pilasters of the same design but of slightly greater height, and the same curved string

167

course as that seen over the niche containing the Virgin is repeated over each of the upper windows. Otherwise the exterior is very restrained and the composition is enlivened by the play of light across the complicated system of tiled roofs.

A narrow entrance hall leads through the clergy house and gives access to the body of the church. But to enable pilgrims to circulate freely through the church, larger doors were provided, leading straight outside, from the first bay of the nave. The strong longitudinal axis and the narrow choir and sanctuary are typical of the Vorarlberg tradition, but the interior is unusual in several respects, particularly in its open plan. Peter Thumb abandoned the normal system of wall pillars and instead replaced the traditional heavy vault by a light and almost flat vault constructed only of plaster and laths on a timber frame. This meant that he could dispense with any internal or external buttressing and could make the structure as light and airy as possible. He may have taken his cue from the designs for Rococo libraries, and the motif of the balcony or gallery cantilevered out from the walls and undulating round the interior was used by him in the library of the monastery of St Peter in the Black Forest in 1738. Here at Birnau the gallery divides the church into two storeys; these are treated separately, each with its own order of pilasters.

There is a revealing contrast between this interior and that of Zwiefalten in the relationship between the structure and the decoration. At Zwiefalten the *rocaille* decoration is applied to a relatively orthodox solid structure in such profusion that its integrity is deliberately broken down, but at Birnau there is no sense of solid structure whatsoever. Architectural elements and decorative elements have become one and the same thing, and the observer ceases to look for a rational construction where the structural elements are precisely defined. Fantasy reigns supreme and the pilgrim passes into an irrational fairy-tale world intended as a foretaste of heaven.

In the nave vault frescoes, painted stucco and fictive stucco are combined together into a single homogeneous whole, and this same sense of overall unity pervades the entire church. Part of the effect is due to the extremely strong lighting in the church from the two levels of windows, uninterrupted by piers and side chapels, and this is reinforced by the whiteness and pale colours of the stucco. But equally important is the scenographic planning. The choir is narrower than the nave, and the sanctuary in turn is

Peter Thumb abandoned the normal system of wall-pillars and replaced the traditional heavy vault by a high and almost flat vault constructed of timber and plaster. This enabled him to create a completely open interior lit by two tiers of large windows, which are divided by the gallery winding its way round the entire interior of the church.

narrower still. This scheme enabled Peter Thumb to flank the entrance to each space with side altars. This means that the high altar is approached through two pairs of side altars and so forms the climax of a cumulative theatrical effect, since all five altars are seen almost full-face by the pilgrim in the nave. But, unlike the Baroque scenographic planning described earlier, there is no passing through strongly differentiated areas of light and shade.

Gottfried Bernhard Göz painted the series of vault frescoes in 1749–50 following a particularly elaborate programme. He was a native of Moravia, born at Velehrad in 1708, but he had studied at Augsburg from 1730, becoming a master there in 1733 and rapidly

Above, a detail of Gottfried Bernhard Göz's nave fresco, showing the plans of the new church being presented to the abbots of Salem who were responsible for the building of the new church.

Left, the strongly illusionistic architectural setting of Göz's nave fresco is most unusual for the date, 1749–50, and almost certainly reflects the influence of the Bohemian painter Václav Vavřinec Reiner.

*Left, Göz's fresco over the choir, painted
1749–50. If the worshipper stands in the right
spot on the floor of the church, he can see his face
reflected in the mirror included in the fresco,
and so participate in the sacred mystery enacted
above.*

establishing for himself an important position in Southern Germany.
His tendency to use heavy brown shadows should be compared to
Spiegler, but at Birnau it makes the frescoes rather too heavy in
relation to the very light interior. The strongly illusionistic architectural settings, looking back to C. D. Asam and others, also
strike an almost old-fashioned note, and it may be argued that his
frescoes are not entirely worthy of the remainder of the church.
Göz began the cycle, most suitably, with a group of angel musicians
over the organ and a large angelic messenger as the bearer of the
good news, while the main fresco over the nave is devoted to the
Virgin as Queen of Heaven, Patroness of the Cistercian Order
and the Comforter of the Distressed.

In the choir, the subject is apocalyptic and a great deal more
esoteric, with the Virgin as *Mater Pulchrae Dilectionis et Timoris et
Agnitionis et Sanctae Spei,* which might be rendered as 'The Mother
of all Beautiful Desires, Timidity, Understanding and Holy Hope'!
Below this fresco in the pendentives are painted *grisaille* figures
representing the four continents, and finally over the high altar
Göz painted Esther before Ahasuerus with the Virgin as Intercessor

*Opposite, the High Altar enshrining the early
15th-century miraculous figure of the Virgin,
for which the church was built. Joseph Anton
Feuchtmayer designed the altar and modelled the
figures of Joachim and Anna, and Zacharias
and Elizabeth in 1749, but the alabaster relief
behind the Virgin is a later insertion by Johann
Georg Wieland, 1790.*

173

Above, the famous Honigschlecker *or Honey Licker, by Joseph Anton Feuchtmayer, carries a beehive in humorous allusion to St Bernard of Clairveaux on whose altar he stands.*

Left, the Virgin and Child group which is the focal point of the whole church. In the early 15th century the original miraculous Virgin was replaced by this group, but it was not until the early 18th century that the monks of Salem decided to build a special church to house it on their own land at Birnau.

before Christ at the Last Judgement. This last fresco is an example of the popular device of combining the Old Testament prefiguration of a scene with that scene itself.

The most ingenious and novel idea in the church is included in the choir fresco. There the Christ Child is enshrined in the belly of the Virgin of the Immaculate Conception and a beam of light connects him with the flaming heart held by the figure of Piety. The heart is connected in turn by a second beam of light to a real mirror set in the plaster and 'held' by a putto. If the pilgrim stations himself on the correct spot in the church he can see his face reflected in the mirror and so participate in the sacred mystery enacted above. Further, he is also the personal recipient through Piety of the divine inspiration of the Christ Child—a remarkable and totally unprecedented conceit.

The third member of the trio who created Birnau was the sculptor and stuccoist Joseph Anton Feuchtmayer, and he worked in the church from 1748 until 1758, assisted in the last years by Johann Georg Dirr. Feuchtmayer belonged to the famous Bavarian family of stucco artists from Wessobrun, who spelt their name in a variety of different ways and included Johann Michael Feichtmayr. He was born at Linz in 1696, and at first he was brought up at Schongau in Bavaria, but from 1706 his father, Franz Joseph, was active at Salem. Joseph Anton, however, probably gained most from his activity under the sculptor and stuccoist Diego Antonio Carlone at Weingarten in the years 1718–25, and by the beginning of the second quarter of the century he had emerged as the most important sculptor in the area of Lake Constance.

Feuchtmayer's personality is indelibly stamped on all the sculpture in the church, and his strongly twisted poses and almost Mannerist distortions are wedded to a robust realism with results that sometimes verge on the grotesque. St Elizabeth and St Anne on the high altar with their long muscular necks are somewhat disturbing in their brilliant observation of some of the less attractive features of old age, but they have a poignancy and utter sincerity that is fully in sympathy with the homely quality of the entire interior. In displaying these qualities Joseph Anton Feuchtmayer is as much acting as the heir to the great tradition of German Gothic wood carving as he is consciously exploiting the qualities of the Rococo. His is essentially the art of a country craftsman of genius entirely uninhibited by any intellectual considerations.

However it is in the robust putti that populate the church, that

Anna modelled in hard stucco by Joseph Anton Feuchtmayer in 1749. Her long muscular neck verges on the grotesque, but she has a poignancy and utter sincerity which is entirely in sympathy with the homely quality of the interior.

175

Left, Joseph Anton Feuchtmayer carved the series of Stations of the Cross from wood in 1753. They are conspicuous for the exquisite sensitivity of the detail and the absolute harmony between the figures and the rocaille *elements.*

Right, the High Altar is approached through two pairs of side altars and is thus the climax of a cumulative theatrical effect. All five altars are seen almost full face by the pilgrim in the nave, but there is none of the dramatic lighting favoured by the Baroque architects.

Feuchtmayer reaches the peak of his achievement, and these have a wit and vitality unrivalled in the churches previously described. Justly famous is the superb *Honigschlecker*, or Honey Licker, which stands by the altarpiece dedicated to St Bernard of Clairvaux; this putto carries a beehive in witty allusion to the saint. The gesture of the plump little fellow licking his finger is further illustrated by the angry bees swarming out of the hive, and these are also to be found on the *scagliola* frame of the altarpiece. Wit, realism and an intense humanity are the hallmarks of the putti of Joseph Anton Feuchtmayer.

In 1750 the sculpture for the altars was complete, but Feuchtmayer and his studio continued work on the fittings for the church. Perhaps the finest of these is the series of Stations of the Cross, which he carved in 1753; these are conspicuous both for the exquisite sensitivity of the carving and the absolute harmony between the figures and the *rocaille* elements. The cartouches are carved with settings in low relief, but these spread out over the frames to form the supports for the deeply moving *tableaux*, carved in the round and painted in naturalistic colours. Assisted by Georg Dirr, Feuchtmayer was also responsible in 1757 for the series of 18 gilt busts that decorate the galleries. Each of these is accompanied by a putto carrying the appropriate attribute, but in those executed by Dirr, including Christ and the Virgin, there is an almost courtly elegance and refinement which is totally foreign to Feuchtmayer. However, despite a few later alterations, Birnau remains one of the most complete and harmonious expressions of the Rococo in the whole of Southern Germany.

176

Steinhausen and Die Wies

Above, when first built, 1727–33, the pilgrimage church of Steinhausen stood isolated in the country, but now a small village clusters round it. The strongly pronounced verticality is unusual for Dominikus Zimmermann, and the delicately curved outlines of the gables give the church a more pronounced Rococo flavour than Birnau.

The churches of Steinhausen and Die Wies have been coupled together in this chapter for a number of reasons, not least because they were both designed and decorated by the Zimmermann brothers. Both too are pilgrimage churches built in the depths of the country, but above all they represent the most highly developed Rococo churches to survive. Steinhausen is located in that area of Upper Swabia that now forms part of Württemberg, and it has been a pilgrimage shrine since the 15th century. During the 17th century, the number of pilgrims increased until in 1727 Didacus Ströbele, the abbot of the Premonstratensian abbey of Schussenried to which Steinhausen belonged, decided to rebuild the church on a much larger scale. Dominikus Zimmermann was called in as architect and in 1733 the new church was consecrated, although the altars were not finished until considerably later.

Basically the plan of the church consists of a large longitudinal oval nave with a small transverse oval choir and a narrow entrance passage flanked by staircases at the west end, but the exterior is so squared off as to make the oval plan almost invisible from the outside. In fact, the most conspicuous feature of the exterior is the strong verticality of the structure, articulated as it is with the flat giant pilasters painted a light green in contrast to the yellow walls. Over the west end rises the simple and elegant tower, while the roof system bears little relationship to the organisation within. The central and highest roof over the nave is closed by high gable forms, and from this four simple lower roofs join up with the tower and the gable of the east end and the gables of the transverse axis. These give the church an elongated quasi-Greek cross plan, and it is not until the church is entered that the visitor realises that the

Left, the oval central space dominates the entire composition and the ten slender columns supporting the vault allow the sunlight to flood the whole interior. However, the dark green and red side altars and pulpit, by Joachim Früholzer, strike a sombre and alien note in this joyous interior.

gables have no structural significance and that the windows in them only light the roof space. However the delicately curved outlines of these gables and the light decorative use made of the pilasters, together with the abstract shapes of the upper windows, give the exterior of the church a much more pronounced Rococo flavour than Birnau.

Inside, the emphasis is again on height with ten slender piers articulating the main oval space and supporting the shallow vault. Below the level of the capitals the decoration is very restrained and almost entirely confined to the altars and furnishings, whose dark colours are in direct contrast to the brilliant white plaster of the walls and piers. Joachim Früholzer was responsible for the dark green and red side altars and pulpit (1746) and the high altar (1749–50), but although these are of undoubted high quality, they are totally out of sympathy with the work of the Zimmermanns, and it is above the levels of the capitals that the real significance of Steinhausen is to be found.

Below, Dominikus Zimmermann so squared off the exterior of Steinhausen that the oval interior comes as a complete surprise. As at Birnau, the pilgrims circulated through the pair of doors at the west end of the side aisles rather than through the tower door.

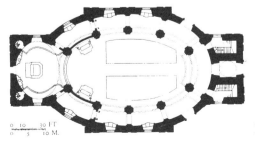

Left, Johann Baptist Zimmermann's fresco over the nave at Steinhausen, 1730–31. The frame round the fresco has vanished and instead the stucco decorations form a parapet beyond which is seen the visionary world of the fresco.

Opposite, the interior of the choir of Die Wies with the entrance flanked by the pulpit and the Abbot of Steingaden's 'box'. Zimmermann pierced the vaulting over the choir arcades to allow more light into the choir from the upper windows of the galleries.

Below, a detail of one of the capitals. Naturalistic details such as flowers and sheep's heads are included.

The great fresco over the nave, painted by Johann Baptist Zimmermann in 1730–31, depicts the Four Corners of the Earth paying homage to the Virgin as Queen of Heaven. She is surrounded by saints and angels in the clouds while groups of figures symbolising the Four Corners of the Earth are depicted on the margin of the fresco, standing in the almost continuous landscape that extends round the vault. The end sections are occupied by Adam and Eve in the Garden of Eden, and the Fountain of Life, and both of these are flanked by groves of trees. Here it is difficult to believe that this was one of the first major frescoes to be painted by Zimmermann, and that he had only taken up painting after he had reached the age of 50. The brilliance and fluency of his free handling of pale colours and the gentle lyrical tone of his frescoes made him much the most influential Rococo fresco painter in Southern Germany, and it is hardly surprising that he was heavily in demand to assist Cuvilliés at Nymphenburg and elsewhere.

Dominikus Zimmermann headed the team of Wessobrunn stuccoists who decorated the church, and, as at Birnau, the decoration follows the 'Bavarian' rather than the 'French' manner, with only the most important parts picked out in gold. Unlike the contemporary decorations by the Asam brothers, the frame round the fresco has vanished and instead the stucco decorations form a parapet beyond which is seen the visionary world of the fresco. The short sections of balustrade surmounted by urns reinforce the illusion, and above the organ the Garden of Eden stretches away into the distance. At Zwiefalten the junction between the fresco and the stucco is masked by the riot of *rocaille* elements running into the painted area, but there was no clearly defined

Left, the interior of Steinhausen. On top of the columns Dominikus Zimmermann placed a series of ten seated figures of Apostles (St Peter and St Paul are included in the High Altar) and these act as a link between the pilgrims below and the heavenly world above.

The church of Die Wies still lies isolated in the fields; attached to the choir is the tower and the twin blocks of the clergy house. Dominikus Zimmermann grouped the windows together in decorative patterns of abstract shapes, picked out in white against the yellow walls.

relationship between the two. At Steinhausen Zimmermann approached the problem differently and broke down the barrier by clearly defining the fresco and the stuccoes as different parts of the same single visionary world. The pilgrims in the body of the church look up to the stucco figures of the Apostles seated on the tops of the piers, and these, by virtue of their crude realism and cheerful colours belong to both worlds and act as intercessors on behalf of the pilgrims below.

Much greater use is made of naturalistic elements than at Birnau and these are inserted into the stucco decorations with an almost playful abandon. Flowers and sheep's heads are included in the capitals, while elsewhere sprays of flowers are found to be visited by beetles and other insects, all modelled in stucco and painted in lively colours. But perhaps most charming of all is the pair of doves cooing at each other in one of the upper windows near the choir entrance.

Steinhausen acts as a prelude to Die Wies and many of the ideas found there, such as the abstract shapes of the windows, are developed to the full in the later church, although the unrestrained joy in the world of nature expressed at Steinhausen is unfortunately lost. Die Wies was not begun until 1745, for the miracle that occasioned it only occurred in 1738. The story is worth telling for the light it casts on the fervour of the times, since the total cost of 180,000 florins was raised in a few years almost entirely from simple pilgrims. The church was constructed as a shrine to house the sculpture called the Flagellated Saviour, which had been made by two monks of the monastery of Steingaden from fragments of several wooden figures of saints. They had covered the joints with canvas and painted it in gruesome colours, and the figure used to be carried round in procession on Good Fridays. However, it so frightened the local inhabitants that in 1734 it was put away in

Groundplan of Die Wies. As at Steinhausen, Zimmerman employed a longitudinal plan for the nave, but here the choir is made into a more important spatial unit.

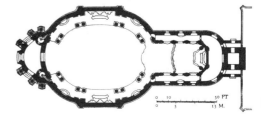

183

the garret of a house at Steingaden, only to be taken away four years later to a farm at Die Wies. On the night of 14 June 1738 at evening prayers tears were seen in the eyes, and this was the beginning of the pilgrimages to Die Wies, which rapidly grew in popularity. In 1740 a small chapel was built, but this was soon inadequate, and in 1745 Dominikus Zimmermann was called in to build a splendid new pilgrimage church and the attached clergy house, which was also to be the summer residence of the Abbot of Steingaden.

Like Steinhausen the basic plan of Die Wies is based on a longitudinal oval with the vault of the main space carried on free-standing pillars. To this oval is attached a strongly convex façade, which allows space for a low semicircular entrance hall with an organ gallery above, and, opposite it, a deep sanctuary surrounded by a gallery and linked to the clergy house by the single tower. The simple, tall piers of Steinhausen are replaced by coupled pillars of an unusual design, since each of the four sides consists of a broad convex surface flanked by narrow concave strips. Above, the forms of the arches supporting the vault are also heavily modified, and the smooth segmental arches of Steinhausen are replaced by abstract shapes with *rocaille* protrusions. Both of

The extreme crudity of the miraculous figure of Christ scourged gives it a macabre quality, enhanced by the sickening shade of green it is painted.

184

Left, the clumped red scagliola columns form part of the structure of the church as well as that of the High Altar. Ägid Verhelst the Elder carved the figures of the Evangelists.

these innovations succeed in their intention of reducing the structural qualities of the pillars and arches to the bare minimum and the eye can no longer, as at Steinhausen, follow clearly defined structural forms. Instead, even the pillars take on the rich decorative quality of icing sugar. Once again the stuccoes round the base of the shallow vault are treated as a light parapet, beyond which is to be seen the limitless sky and the preparations for the Last Judgement, painted by Johann Baptist Zimmermann. At Steinhausen the unreal insubstantial world began above the level of the capitals, but at Die Wies it takes over the entire church.

Dominikus Zimmermann grouped the windows together into decorative patterns of abstract shapes, and on the exterior of the church these are picked out in white against the yellow walls, while pilasters and additional white decorative bands add to the

Above, St Jerome, one of the Four Fathers of the Latin Church carved by Anton Sturm, 1753–54, to decorate the coupled columns supporting the main vault. The nervous brittle energy of the figure is entirely in sympathy with the decoration of that area of the church.

Above left, the congregation space at Die Wies with the great vault fresco by Johann Baptist Zimmermann depicting the preparations for the Last Judgement.

185

rich effect. Inside, the influence of the Zimmermann's activity with Cuvilliés in the 1730s becomes apparent in the far greater use of gilding than at Steinhausen and the much smaller number of naturalistic motifs painted in lively colours. The use of colour has changed and becomes a great deal more theatrical, partly under the influence of the Asams. The nave is decorated in white and gold with little colour other than that provided by the fresco and pulpit; this is in deliberate contrast to the red *scagliola* columns of the high altar and the bright blue *scagliola* columns separating the sanctuary from the gallery. The gilding too is richer, and the sanctuary becomes the visual climax of the church. Architecturally this area is treated almost as a hall church with the galleries designed as aisles extending to the full height of the sanctuary. Zimmermann exploited this scheme by piercing the lower parts of the vault so that additional light pours into the sanctuary from the upper windows of the galleries, and the blue columns thus at first support a lace-work of *rocaille* stucco instead of a solid vault.

The wooden framework on which Die Wies is constructed freed the Zimmermanns almost completely from structural worries, and in the sanctuary this freedom is pushed to its logical conclusion. Irrationality and the negation of structural integrity is taken to extremes; for example, the sections of entablature carried by the free-standing columns flanking the high altar have their corners extended and rolled up like curls of toffee. The relatively indifferent quality of Balthasar Augustin Albrecht's altarpiece and of the sculpture by Ägid Verhelst the elder does not detract from the overwhelming ensemble, while the superb figures of the Fathers of the Latin Church in the nave by Anton Sturm have a brittle nervous energy that is entirely in sympathy with the decoration of that area of the church. Here, in contrast to Steinhausen, the Zimmermanns were able to complete the fittings of the church also, and Dominikus's pulpit is one of his most splendid and lyrical creations. Instead of a *tableau* Dominikus struck on the very ingenious idea of a special 'box' to balance the pulpit and from there it was intended that the abbot should follow the services, out of the gaze of the pilgrims. Dominikus Zimmermann died at Die Wies in 1766, close to his masterpiece, and after recent restorations the church has been returned to a state as close as possible to that of the time when it was completed by him. Die Wies may have been praised uncritically in the past, but it remains today the triumphant climax to the Rococo churches of Southern Germany.

The pulpit of Die Wies, designed by Dominikus Zimmermann. One of his most splendid and lyrical creations, the pulpit illustrates the theme of the Pentecostal Storm accompanying the Holy Spirit.

Further reading list

Bourke, John, *Baroque Churches of Central Europe*; London, 1962

Hempel, Eberhard, *Baroque Art and Architecture in Central Europe*; Harmondsworth, 1965

Knox, Brian, *Bohemia and Moravia – An Architectural Companion*; London, 1962

Lees-Milne, James, *Baroque in Italy*; London, 1959

Pevsner, Nikolaus, *An Outline of European Architecture*; Harmondsworth, 1960

Sitwell, Sacheverell, *German Baroque Art*; London, 1927

Wittkower, Rudolph, *Art and Architecture in Italy, 1600–1750*; Harmondsworth, 1965

Glossary

aedicule motif: a framing motif normally consisting of an entablature and pediment supported by two columns.

atlantid: a massive male figure replacing a column or pier.

caryatid: a female figure replacing a column.

clerestory: the upper order of windows in a fully developed Gothic nave.

coffering: the patterning of a vault with recessed square or polygonal panels, originally structural in function.

finial: a decorative motif applied to the top of a building.

fresco: a technique of painting in which the pigment is applied to fresh wet plaster.

helm: the decorative finial often known popularly as an 'onion dome' applied to the top of a Baroque tower, particularly in Germany and Austria.

ohrmuschel decoration: a fantastic form of decoration based on the abstract and flowing shapes of ears, pieces of shells, etc., popular from the late 16th until the mid-17th century.

Palladian motif: a triple opening where the central space is taller and closed by an arch, and the side openings are narrower and closed by flat entablatures acting as lintels.

pediment: a triangular or segmental form bounded by mouldings; originally the gable end of a temple but later used as a decorative motif.

pendentive: of similar function to a squinch except that the structure here is solid and faired in.

piano nobile: the principal floor, usually the first or above, of a house, specifically an Italian palace.

pier: a solid structural element between windows, doors or other openings.

pilaster: a column in relief attached to a wall, mainly decorative in function.

platzlgewolbe: a hemispherical vault dissected by four semicircular or segmental arches to give a square or rectangular plan.

quoins: decorative handling of the external corners of a building, usually rusticated.

rustication: masonry in which either the individual stones are given a rough texture or the joints are emphasised.

scagliola: a fake marble made of hard plaster polished to an almost mirror-like surface with an infinite range of colours, more versatile than real marble.

squinch: an arch inserted across the corner of a space to carry a vault above.

wall-pillars: piers forming a solid wall attached to the outside wall, characteristic of the Vorarlberg type of church design.

Index

Acknowledgements

Key to picture positions: (*T*) *top,* (*B*) *bottom,* (*L*) *left,* (*R*) *right. Numbers refer to pages on which the pictures appear.*

Alinari: 18(*L*), 66, 79. Anderson: 21, 55(*B*), 60(*R*). Anderson-Viollet: 17(*T*). Lala Aufsberg: 29. Wilfried Bahnmüller-Bavaria: 52. Barnaby's Picture Library: 36(*R*), 37. Emil Bauer: 118, 144, 147, 178. Emil Bauer-Bavaria: 124, 138. Bayerisches Landsamt für Denkmalplege, Munich: 126. G. Berengo-Gardin: 91. E. Boudot-Lamotte: 44(*L*), 83(*T*), 123(*T*), 184(*L*). Trustees of the British Museum: 63(*R*), 75. Dominique Buigné-Rapho: 26. Courtauld Institute: 63(*BL*). Deutsche Photothek, Dresden: 118, 183(*L*). Josef Ehm: 38(*B*), 117, 120. Fotografia Ferruzzi: 84, 85, 86, 87, 92(*L*), 92(*R*). Gabinetto Fotografico Nazionale: 13. Germanisches Nationalmuseum, Nuremberg: 125. Graphische Sammlung Albertina: 67(*R*), 70(*R*), 74(*T*), 74(*B*). Leo Gundermann: 137(*T*). Hamlyn Group Archives: 88. Prof. Hege-Bavaria: 34(*R*). Dr Hell-Bavaria: 156. Hermann Hessler: 142, 148, 149(*T*), 158, 162, 164, 166, 169, 170, 171, 172, 173, 174(*L*), 175, 176, 184(*R*), 185(*L*), 185(*R*), 186. Hirmer Fotoarchiv: 42, 49, 128, 133. Franz Höch: 129, 130, 131, 132, 134. Robert Holder-Bavaria: 181(*R*). Jos. Jeiter: 10, 16(*L*), 34(*L*), 56(*T*), 67(*L*), 68, 72, 78, 153. A. F. Kersting: 27(*L*), 28, 40, 48, 50, 97(*L*), 99, 102, 103, 140, 141, 149(*B*), 177. H. Koepf: 137(*B*), 167. Le Brun-Bavaria: 180. Mansell-Anderson: 11, 12(*T*), 20, 76. Bildarchiv Foto Marburg: 17(*B*), 19, 31, 32, 35(*R*), 38(*T*), 41(*R*), 46(*L*), 47, 60(*L*), 63(*T*), 127(*T*). Ampliaciones y Reproducciones MAS: 98(*L*), 98(*R*). Erwin Meyer: 106(*L*), 106(*R*), 108, 109, 110, 111, 112, 113. Riccardo Moncalvo: 100(*T,L*), 101. Erich Müller: 41(*B*), 45, 115, 119, 122, 123(*B*), 155, 161. Office du Livre, Fribourg: 116(*R*), 152. Österreichische Nationalbibliothek: 105(*BL*), 105(*BR*). Oscar Poss-Bavaria: 46(*R*). Mauro Pucciarelli: 64. RIBA: 93, 97(*L*), 100(*BL*). Roger-Viollet: 23(*B*). Scala: 94, 121, 163. Helga Schmidt-Glassner: 35(*L*), 36(*L*), 44(*R*), 116(*L*), 179(*L*). Toni Schneiders: 27(*R*), 43, 157, 159, 174(*R*), 181(*L*), 182. Toni Schneiders-Bavaria: 150. Soprintendenza ai Monumenti del Piemonte: 23(*T*), 96(*B*), 100(*R*). Staatliches Museum, Schwerin: 15. Vic Stacey: 25. Teuffen-Bavaria: 145. A. Vasari & Figlio: 12(*B*), 16(*R*), 55(*T*), 56(*B*), 58(*T*), 59(*T*), 59(*B*), 61, 71, 77. Leonard von Matt: 8, 70(*L*), 80, 81. Alexander and Elizabeth Wengraf: 105(*T*).

Plans on pages 107, 127(*B*), 179(*R*) and 18(*R*) are from E. Hempel: *Baroque Art and Architecture in Central Europe,* and those on pages 18(*R*), 54 and 83(*B*) from R. Wittkower: *Art and Architecture in Italy: 1600 to 1750,* both published by Penguin Books Ltd.

189

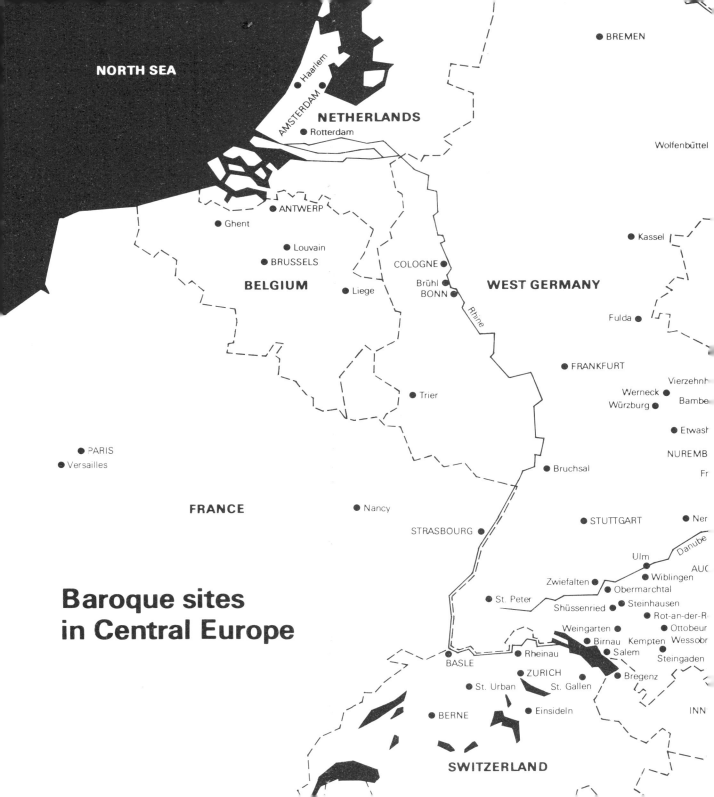

Baroque sites in Central Europe

NORTH SEA

NETHERLANDS

Haarlem
AMSTERDAM
Rotterdam

BREMEN

Wolfenbüttel

ANTWERP
Ghent
Louvain
BRUSSELS
BELGIUM
Liege

COLOGNE
Brühl
BONN
WEST GERMANY
Rhine

Kassel

Fulda

FRANKFURT

Vierzehnh
Werneck
Würzburg
Bambe

Etwash

Trier

NUREMB
Fr

PARIS
Versailles

Bruchsal

FRANCE

Nancy

STUTTGART
Ner

STRASBOURG

Ulm
Danube
AU(

Zwiefalten
Obermarchtal
Shüssenried
Steinhausen
Wiblingen
Rot-an-der-R
Ottobeur
Wessobr

St. Peter

Weingarten
Birnau
Kempten
Salem
Steingaden

BASLE
Rheinau
ZURICH
St. Urban
St. Gallen
Bregenz

BERNE
Einsideln
INN

SWITZERLAND